Summarizing, Paraphrasing, and Retelling

Skills for Better Reading, Writing, and Test Taking

Emily Kissner

HEINEMANN
Portsmouth, NH

Heinemann

361 Hanover Street
Portsmouth, NH 03801–3912
www.heinemann.com

Offices and agents throughout the world

Library of Congress Cataloging-in-Publication Data
Kissner, Emily.
    Summarizing, paraphrasing, and retelling : skills for better reading,
writing, and test taking / Emily Kissner.
       p. cm.
    Includes bibliographical references.
    ISBN 0-325-00797-7 (alk. paper)
    1. Reading comprehension. 2. English language—Composition
and exercises—Study and teaching. I. Title.

LB1050.45.K47 2006
372.47—dc22   2005028402

Editor: Danny Miller
Production service: Denise A. Botelho
Production coordinator: Sonja S. Chapman
Cover design: Jenny Jensen Greenleaf
Compositor: Gina Poirier
Manufacturing: Louise Richardson

Printed in the United States of America on acid-free paper
17 16 15   VP   10 11 12

Contents

List of Forms

Acknowledgments

To thank my husband, Stephen Kissner, for his help on this book is an understatement. Without his encouragement, comments, and support, this book would not exist and my classroom would be a very different place. He is the most gifted teacher I know, and his fourth graders are lucky indeed. When I came up with a new idea for teaching summarizing, he was always willing to try it out in his classroom and provide me with valuable feedback. This is as much his project as it is mine.

Dinnertime conversations with my family never stray far from teaching. My mother and father, Charles and Karen Pearce, are both teachers as well. They have helped me in so many ways, from talking through difficult ideas to watching our two young sons while we worked on writing.

I would also like to thank my colleagues at Biglerville Elementary, particularly Karen Daugherty, Tina McGough, and Megan McLean. Their support has been invaluable as I made the transition from middle school to elementary school. Rolland Kiracofe, who originally hired me to teach at Northwest Middle School, set my teaching career in motion. I will always be grateful for his kindness and encouragement.

Finally, I would like to thank all of the people that I worked with at Heinemann. I wrote this book with a laptop balanced in one hand and a baby held in the other, and I am so grateful for everyone's help, support, and kindness during a hectic time. I would especially like to thank editor Danny Miller for his wonderful advice and comments.

Introduction

I started teaching language arts at the height of the whole language movement. The supervisor in my district had removed the old scope and sequence, drill and kill–based curriculum in favor of a far more open curriculum that allowed teachers to plan their own lessons and make their own judgments. "But I have no judgment!" I remember wailing to my mother, also a teacher. "How do you think I learned what to do?" she asked, and showed me her bookshelf, which was covered with stacks and stacks of professional books. I got the message. I couldn't expect to make it through a career of teaching with only the knowledge I had picked up in a handful of undergraduate courses. If I was going to be successful, I needed to read. And read. And read.

During the next few years, I amassed my own collection of books. When I came to a thorny patch in my instruction—for example, how to get students to apply grammar skills to their writing—I would look through the books for ideas and solutions. If I didn't find the answer in my own books, I would borrow from my mother's bookshelf or the reading specialist's. I knew that I couldn't become comfortable with every aspect of teaching reading and writing in one year, so I slowly built on my knowledge base and developed my own judgment.

This helped me to cope with the changes that swept through my classroom during the course of the next seven years. I started teaching seventh grade writing, then added sixth grade writing to the mix. When Integrated Language Arts came to our school a few years later, I was thrilled to be able to teach a ninety-minute block of reading and writing. Our state outcomes became content standards, our state testing program was transformed from performance-based assessment to "selected response," or multiple choice, and the district middle school reading and writing department was headed by three different supervisors who dispersed three different curriculum manuals. As if these changes were not enough, I uprooted myself after seven years and went to teach a self-contained sixth grade class in a tiny rural district. Moving from a district with 28,000 students to a district with 1,800 was quite a culture shock.

Some people may have found the pace frustrating, but I liked the excitement. I learned how to adapt to new thinking and new ideas while still holding on to the philosophies and structures that worked in my classroom. The more things changed, the more I could see how some things remained the same. Whether I was teaching to outcomes or standards, whether my curriculum was organized according to theme or genre, whether I had a classroom with windows, I faced young adolescents every day. All the books in the world cannot prepare a teacher for what happens once the students walk into the room.

I certainly wasn't prepared to teach summarizing. Included as a content standard and an assessment anchor, I knew that summarizing was important, and I dutifully tried to help my sixth and seventh graders write summaries of both fiction and nonfiction texts. I envisioned smoothly written short pieces, like those in *TV Guide*, that would elegantly capture the essence of a text with a minimum of words.

What I got were stacks of bizarre constructions that claimed to be summaries—or "sumeries," as my students often wrote—that either copied whole sentences of text, focused on just one section, or missed the main points altogether. Sometimes I wondered if the students had read the same text that I had. The more able students could occasionally pull together a coherent comment or two, but often they would try to jam a summary into the traditional paragraph template—topic sentence, supporting details, concluding sentence.

> I learned many things from the article. How tomb robbers took things from tombs, what they stole from tombs, and what they were like. It was a great article.

I wasn't sure of how to help them. My usual comments— "Elaborate. Add more. Give more detail"—are not helpful for summarizing. The students thought I had become temporarily insane when I told them, "That's too long. Make it short. Are those details necessary?"

Standing in front of the classroom with a student summary on the overhead projector, I struggled to explain to the students why it was not effective.

"But the article is about trees, right?" Patrick asked from the front row. "So why can't I say, 'This article is about trees?'"

I floundered. As the teacher, I was supposed to know these things! "It's not good writing," I said, finally.

"It sounds good to me," Patrick said, to a chorus of agreement from elsewhere in the room. "I think it's fine."

I tried to use various graphic organizers or catchy formulas, but I couldn't find anything that would work with every text every time. "Write down the main points and important details," I told the students, only to realize that they could not *find* the main points or identify the important details.

To make matters worse, the usual rubric we used to assess reading comprehension questions did not work for summaries. We were focused on getting kids to include text evidence in their responses to questions. However, summaries don't require explicit text evidence or references back to the text, and when kids tried to add those elements, they created some pretty strange responses.

> This article was about tomb robbers in ancient Egypt. I know this because the author made the title be "Tomb Robbers and the Mummy's Treasure." The author explained what treasures were in tombs and how the tomb robbers stole the treasures. I know this because the author said so.

So I was faced with teaching something that I couldn't explain and couldn't assess. It was time to hit the books and find out what was really going on.

Strangely, though, I didn't find very much written about summarizing. There were a few pages in a content area reading textbook, scattered mentions in books about reading strategies, and philosophical ruminations about what is important in a text. Most discussions of summarizing cited the same research and listed the same steps for helping kids to improve their work. I found little to tell me why students don't summarize well, what skills students need to write good summaries, or the relationship between summarizing and reading comprehension.

I knew that summarizing was important. Not only is it included on content standards and tested on yearly assessments, but it is also a skill used in everyday life. But the question remained—how would I teach it?

I expanded my search beyond the usual reference books and into the realm of journal articles. Although there were many articles about summarizing through the mid and late 1980s, the topic dropped off the scene through much of the past fifteen years, relegated to mentions in articles aimed at high school and college teachers.

As teachers and students in my district focused on writing good reading responses and finding text evidence to support their thinking, there was little direct instruction in the skills required for summarizing.

This was and is a shame. The more I learned about summarizing, the more I became convinced that it is a keystone skill for reading. Summarizing deserves more than a brief mention in a language arts curriculum. The ability to summarize is at the heart of comprehension, the very essence of what we want kids to be able to do. A few scattered activities and lists of steps won't help kids to grasp the power of skillful summarizing.

Using what I learned from the journal articles, I worked to break down the skills required for summarizing. There are many! It requires the purposeful synthesis of a number of discrete reading strategies and skills. No wonder my students were having such problems. Many of my colleagues were facing the same problems that I was. "I try to skip through summaries as quickly as I can," another teacher confessed to me. "What is the difference between a summary and a retelling?" someone else asked.

If we want to help our students to become engaged, strategic readers, we must include summarizing instruction in our reading and language arts classrooms. As you will see, summarizing is a skill with far-reaching implications for reading comprehension and content area success. The time spent on teaching summarizing strategies will only help our students to become more efficient, more effective learners.

WHY TEACH SUMMARIZING? 1

Summarizing Is Used in Everyday Life

"What happened in class?" "What was that movie about?" "What was the principal trying to tell us in that email?" These are questions that come up in our daily lives. The answers to these questions require us to sort through details to find the main ideas and sift out trivia. A person who cannot summarize, who cannot select main ideas or invent main idea statements, is adrift in a sea of data, events, and details. Everyone needs to be able to do some rudimentary summarizing to get through life.

Suppose that a new next-door neighbor moves in. The first time you see her, she says that your hair looks like a birds' nest. The next day, she says that your lawn looks like it has been chewed by ferrets and that your house is painted a rather unattractive color. Later she says that the cookies you brought over tasted like dirty feet. How could you summarize your encounters with this neighbor? She's definitely a rude person!

This kind of thinking translates to more subtle encounters. Think about political speeches. Your job as a voter is to find your way through the catchy details and figure out the candidate's main ideas. This is summarizing at its most important. Your ability to think through a speech or platform can affect your life for years to come.

Summarizing Enhances Learning

Studies show that students who write summaries remember the main points of an original text with greater accuracy than students who do not. There have been several studies to test the power of summarizing as a study technique. A college researcher assigned students in a psychology course to three different groups. The control group got to hear a video-taped lecture. One experimental group heard the lecture, but had three four-minute pauses during the lecture to allow time for them to look over their notes. The other experimental group had the same lecture and pauses, but was told to write a summary of the information during each pause. All groups were given both an immediate posttest and a delayed test twelve days later. Both the pause group and the summary group outperformed the control group on both measures. Most important, the summary group's performance did not decrease significantly over the twelve-day gap, and they were better able to recall information from the lecture than the other two groups (Davis and Hult 1997).

In another 1997 study, students who were told to study a text about evolutionary biology to teach the text to a peer by summarizing or explaining outperformed students who were told simply to read the text or listen to a partner's explanation (Coleman, Brown, and Rivkin 1997). Clearly, summaries have a powerful effect on the ability to remember information.

Students who are effective summarizers are also more able to take in and integrate new information. As they look for connections between ideas and find the gist of what they read and hear, they can learn more easily and more effectively (Garner, Gillingham, and White 1989). Many students think of learning as something that just happens when they read a text over and over again. Summarizing strategies provides them with "cognitive shopping bags," as author Rosalie Friend puts it—a way to store incoming ideas efficiently and keep them for future retrieval (Friend 2000).

Summarizing Is a Tool for Measuring Comprehension

Many standardized tests include questions about summaries or main ideas. A summary can give insight into how a student read and understood a text. Although a student with a good understanding of a text will not always write a good summary, a student with a poor understanding of a text can *never* write a good summary.

Most state content standards include some summarizing in one form or another, whether they come right out and say, "Students will write a summary," or "Students will judge main ideas and relevant details in a text." Summaries are often included on state tests. Sometimes students are given the first sentence of a summary and are told to complete it, whereas on other tests students are asked to generate a summary from scratch. Multiple-choice questions also test summarizing skills, with students being asked to choose the sentence that best summarizes the selection, or the information that should be included in a summary.

At the classroom level, teachers can also use summaries as a quick measure of comprehension. Retellings have been used for many years to accomplish this purpose. Summaries, both oral and written, can accomplish the same ends. If students can't recall the important ideas of a selection, chances are they didn't comprehend what they read.

Summarizing can also serve as a "during reading" strategy to help students monitor their own comprehension. Many of my middle-level students falsely equate understanding a text with being able to sound out all the words. "But what did you learn from the text?" I ask, and the students frown and try to change the subject. As I help them to stop at every page or section and try to summarize what came before, they are better able to find the places where their comprehension broke down and are better able to make meaning from what they read.

Chapter Summary

Summarizing is an important skill that is all too often glossed over in the classroom. Summarizing can be used as both an assessment tool and a strategy to enhance comprehension. Most important, summarizing helps us to understand and make meaning of the events of everyday life—what we read, what we view, what we experience. Summarizing is definitely worth learning about.

2

SUMMARIZING, PARAPHRASING, AND RETELLING
Related, But Not the Same

The scene was grim. Eight of us were packed into a cramped, unair-conditioned room, spending the first week of our summer in a kind of curricular sweatshop. Our task was daunting: to unite the previously divided middle school reading and writing programs into one cohesive class. And write 100 days of curriculum in one week, using enough detail so that reading teachers could confidently teach the writing components and writing teachers could teach the reading. The sixth grade table had rapidly devolved into a bizarre reading–writing turf war.

"I don't think retelling is something we want to assess in middle school," a reading specialist said. "I mean, just being able to spit back the characters and plot of a story doesn't show any higher level thinking." To those of us who had taught writing, she said, patronizingly, "One of the goals of teaching reading is to get kids to think critically."

Really.

"Are you talking about retelling or summarizing?" asked a veteran teacher.

"Aren't they both the same thing?" someone else asked.

"If we include retelling—or summarizing—would it be a reading activity or a writing activity?"

"How would we assess it?"

"Well," said one teacher, who came from the more affluent part of the district, "I don't think summarizing is a skill that we should have to teach in middle school. It's time that we stop babying students and expect them to use what they learned in elementary school."

"Or should have learned," someone else chimed in. Reading teachers and writing teachers united momentarily to agree that students should have already learned basically everything before arriving in middle school.

I've found that there's no way to win one of these arguments. In this case, nothing I could have said would have convinced any of these teachers that they were wrong. (Despite the fact that I was the only one who had actually taught reading and writing together, I was still considered a "writing" teacher, and therefore unable to comprehend reading issues!) This group perpetuated four pervasive myths about the related skills of summarizing, paraphrasing, and retelling.

Myth 1: Summarizing, Paraphrasing, and Retelling Are All the Same

Like many myths, this one has a grain of truth. Summarizing, paraphrasing, and retelling are closely related processes, and the ability to summarize depends on some level of skill with paraphrasing and retelling.

However, each of these processes is important in its own right as a tool for comprehension and discussion. When students know the difference between these skills, they can choose the one they need for each circumstance.

Myth 2: Summarizing Is the Same as Recall

Many reading teachers have downplayed simple recall in recent years. Being able to pick out one detail from a passage doesn't show that a reader has a well-developed understanding of the passage. However, summarizing requires students to comprehend, analyze, and synthesize ideas. This is not just spitting back an answer! The reader processes text in one form, makes judgments about the ideas, and restates the text in a new form. This requires higher level thinking.

Myth 3: Students Should Already Know How to Do This

Summarizing, retelling, and paraphrasing are important skills for readers of all levels, even those in college and beyond. Saying that students should have "learned" these skills in a previous class or grade is like saying that students should have learned how to write in first grade and therefore need no more instruction in the topic. The logic just doesn't work.

A third grade teacher may do an excellent job of working with students to summarize third grade text; but, in eighth grade, text is much more complex. Students who mastered summarizing in third grade may need explicit instruction in meeting the new demands of eighth grade–level text.

Myth 4: Summarizing Is Really an Assessment of Writing, Not Reading

It's a fact of life that we can't look into a student's head and see how she comprehends a text. In this day of large class sizes, we can't always confer with every student, either. There will always need to be some kind of written assessment of reading.

Assessing written work always carries some risks. The surface features of a student's response—that is, the grammar, punctuation, and spelling—can overshadow the ideas. This problem, fortunately, is easily solved. A good rubric can help a teacher focus on just the aspects of a summary that reflect reading comprehension. Even a student who is a poor writer can show an understanding of a text in a written summary.

Many standardized tests have avoided the reading/writing question altogether by putting summary questions into multiple-choice format and asking students to choose the best summary of a passage. This is a way that summarizing can be assessed without intimidating students who may not feel comfortable with writing tasks.

The True Facts About Summarizing, Paraphrasing, and Retelling

Summarizing, paraphrasing, and retelling are important parts of any reading and writing curriculum. Before I could start working with these skills in my classroom, though, I needed to figure out exactly how they fit together. Although summarizing is usually mentioned first, it is actually the last stop on a pathway of increasingly complex skills. This pathway begins with paraphrasing.

Paraphrasing

When students are admonished to "put things in their own words" when taking notes, they are actually being told to paraphrase. Paraphrasing is, quite simply, restating ideas in different words. A reader (or listener) can choose to paraphrase one statement, a group of statements, or an entire passage. This is quite different from retelling and summarizing, both of which require a reader to gain a global picture of the text.

Paraphrasing can be oral or written. Orally, it can be as simple as, "Put my last directions into your own words." A written paraphrase can be much more complex, as students could paraphrase formally written text by rewriting it in an informal style.

So paraphrasing is not that difficult. Another step along the pathway takes us to retelling.

Retelling

Retelling is quite simple. After hearing or reading a story, a child "retells" the events to a listener. Many children will spontaneously retell exciting events, books, or movies to one another (and to any other listener who happens to be within earshot!). In recent years, retelling has become more popular as a tool for both instruction and assessment. Although some books will refer to "written retellings," for the purposes of this book, retelling is considered an oral event.

How does retelling begin? Children develop the ability to tell a story with a logical sequence of events between the ages of two and five (Wagner, Sahlen, and Nettelblat 1999). In fact, story retelling has been recognized as a predictor of which preschoolers will have language delays in first grade (Fazio, Naremore, and Connell 1996). Children who have problems retelling stories seem to be more likely to have problems with reading comprehension in later years.

This information is available because education researchers have a long history of working with retelling. Retelling has been used for years as a dependent variable in reading research experiments. After a researcher has done some intervention—a teaching method, questioning strategy, and so on—and asked students to read a text, the benefits of that intervention are measured by asking the student to retell what was read. The retelling is then scored based on a list of criteria to be included. Some retellings are "cued," with the student prompted to give specific information, either by a story grammar chart or direct questioning. Others are simply given on a free recall basis.

From the education research journals, retelling made its way to the classroom. And with good reason. Retelling is far from being just a regurgitation of facts and events. A 1985 study showed that repeated practice in retelling—even with minimal teacher instruction—improves reading comprehension, with transfer to future reading tasks (Gambrell, Pfeiffer, and Wilson 1985). Retelling is beneficial for students from preschool to college and beyond. Because it is an oral activity, retelling is an excellent bridge from social literacy activities into silent, individual ones. Being able to talk through a story helps children to process what went on, and come to a new understanding of events or information.

I was excited to learn about retelling, because it seemed an easy way to help my students become better readers and writers. I was even more excited to see how the pathway through paraphrasing and retelling led me to my eventual goal: summarizing.

Summarizing

If paraphrasing is just restating ideas, and a retelling is completely oral, what is a summary? This question has plagued researchers—and students—for years. Definitions for a summary abound. It may be most useful to study some of the important characteristics of a summary. Although there are some issues still up for debate, most people agree on the following points.

A summary should be shorter than the original text. How much shorter? It depends. A fifteen-page article could be summarized in one page, two pages, or even a single paragraph, depending on the purpose of the summary and the needs of the audience.

A summary should include the main ideas of the text. Although this sounds easy enough, it's where most students, and most adults, have trouble. Stating the main ideas of a text is easy when the author comes out and states them. The task becomes much more difficult when the main ideas are implicit, or unstated, as is usually the case in fiction.

A summary should reflect the structure and order of the original text. This can become another stumbling block. Fiction text written in chronological order is easiest for students to summarize. When it comes to nonfiction, however, authors use a variety of structures. Most students are used to the form of text that states a main point and then supports that point with details. (That's the structure I've used in most of this book.) However, if a text is written in compare-and-contrast order, the summary should follow suit.

A summary should include important details. "But how do I know which details are important?" students ask, and research shows that adolescents don't always agree with adults on the importance of specific ideas (Garner et al. 1989). But summaries do need to include the details that support an author's main points.

A summary, therefore, is a shortened version of an original text, stating the main ideas and important details of the text with the same text structure and order of the original. It had taken me time, but I could finally lay the myths of summarizing to rest. I knew what summarizing was, how paraphrasing was completely different, and why a retelling and a summary could never be confused. Unfortunately, I didn't learn these things in time for curriculum writing.

The argument at the sixth grade table evaporated as our supervisor came over. "Everything going well?" he asked, and all at the table smiled and nodded.

"You know," said the reading specialist, after he left, "we only have to write 100 days worth of lessons. We could always leave it up to the individual teachers whether or not to teach summarizing."

Another teacher nodded. "That way, those of us with—uh, more advanced kids—can move on to lessons that will really benefit them." She looked pointedly at me.

"Besides," someone else said, "if we were going to have summarizing tasks, we'd need to have anchor papers, rubrics, assessments—it's just too much work."

Actually, I was glad of their decision. It gave me the freedom to spend the next few years teaching summarizing on my own, working through the myths and misconceptions, and developing some pretty good lessons. Before I could go back and teach my students, though, I needed to settle the question: What makes a good summary?

Chapter Summary

- Although summarizing, paraphrasing, and retelling are related, they are somewhat different in process, form, and product.

- A summary is a shortened version of an original text. A summary should include all main ideas and important details, while reflecting the structure and order of the original.

- A reader paraphrases by restating ideas from a text in a new way.

- Retelling is orally restating what is remembered from the text.

3 WHAT DOES A GOOD SUMMARY LOOK LIKE?

A summary conveys the gist of a piece of text. When well written, a summary has a kind of elegance. Like a piece of Shaker furniture, its lines are spare and minimal, with not a word out of place or without function. Not only does the reader understand what's going on in the text, but he or she is able to express that awareness with an economy of words.

How can we explain what a good summary looks like? Over the years, researchers like Brown and Day (1983) have looked at successful summaries and have identified some basic rules:

1. Include important ideas.

2. Delete trivia.

3. Delete repeated ideas.

4. Collapse lists.

5. Choose or create a topic sentence.

Teaching summaries should be easy, then—just list the rules, make students memorize them, and they'll be fine. However, we all know that just telling children what the rules are doesn't mean that they know how to apply them. Like many other literacy skills, the ability to write a summary is developmental.

Every summary begins with a piece of text. Nonfiction texts are usually more difficult for students to summarize than fiction texts, probably because students are more familiar with the structure of fiction. For that reason, this chapter focuses on the rules for summarizing expository text.

The next pages present a simple article similar to what my sixth grade students can read independently. When I can't find a text to suit my purposes in the classroom, I sit down to write my own. I first wrote this

Gardening with Native Plants

What is a native plant?

Native plants are the plants that naturally grow in an area. They are accustomed to the rainfall, temperature, and pests of the region. The wildlife of an area depends on native plants for food and shelter.

But native plants are disappearing. When forests and meadows are bulldozed to build houses and shopping centers, plants are destroyed. The animals that depend on these plants either die or move elsewhere. The U. S. Forest Service reports that when a single plant species becomes extinct, up to 30 other kinds of plants and wildlife are in danger.

You can help by putting native plants in your garden or wildlife habitat. Native plants are great to grow. Once they are established, they don't need lots of water and chemicals to stay healthy. And putting in native plants may attract wildlife to the area as well. For example, monarch butterflies are attracted to milkweed. So when we put native plants into our garden, we're helping animals too.

Choosing native plants

What are the best native plants for your garden? Different plants have different needs. When you go to a nursery to buy plants, read the labels carefully to find out if the plant will thrive in your garden.

Sunlight

Some plants like to bask in the sun all day, while others prefer shade. Look at the information about a plant to find out what it likes.

Full sun—the plant is in direct sunlight for at least 6 hours each day

Partial shade—the plant receives at least 3–6 hours of sun

Full shade—the plant receives less than 3 hours of sun

Moisture

Some plants can't stand to have their roots wet. Find out if your plant likes it wet or dry.

Figure 3–1.

Wet—A plant that likes wet conditions needs a site where it is always wet, even weeks after a rain.

Moist—These plants like the areas that stay soggy for a few days after rain, but eventually dry out.

Dry—If a plant likes dry conditions, it needs a place where the rain quickly dries.

Plant Size

Pay careful attention to the eventual size of a plant. Even though most of the plants look the same size at the nursery, some will stay small, while others could grow taller than your house.

If you are making a wildlife habitat, try to make it as much like a natural forest as you can. Start at the bottom with some low-growing plants to provide shelter for bugs, reptiles, and amphibians. Include some shrubs and understory trees to provide food and cover for birds and squirrels. And don't forget to plant tall-growing canopy trees.

Directions:

In the space below, write a summary of the article. Remember to use the subheadings to help you figure out important ideas.

_____

_____

_____

_____

_____

_____

_____

_____

_____

_____

_____

_____

_____

_____

_____

_____

_____

_____

_____

FIGURE 3–1. *Continued*

article, "Gardening with Native Plants" (Figure 3–1) when I was working with the science teacher to develop a butterfly garden at our school. Before students could research native plants to use for our garden, they needed some idea of what native plants were.

As I wrote the text, I decided to get extra mileage out of it by designing some reading lessons to go with it. The format of the text lent itself to working through the summary rules. As you read the article, try to formulate your own summary. Then, we will work through the rules, looking at how students develop in their understandings of these rules and how they apply them to their own summaries.

Using "Gardening with Native Plants" with Summary Rules
Rule 1: Include Important Ideas

This is the rule that most people associate with summarizing. After all, the purpose of reading is to locate and learn important information. How can this rule pose difficulty for students?

If you work with kids, you've probably learned that they don't always attach importance to the same things that we do. Take the latest round of standardized testing at my school. While I talked to students about the test, I stressed what was important to me—doing one's best, working carefully and accurately, and checking work. My students, on the other hand, had one question that weighed heavily on their minds: Would I let them chew gum during the test, as their teacher had last year? Obviously, we had different ideas of what was important.

When fluent readers interact with a text, they use two different methods to judge whether ideas are important. The first kind of importance, and the kind of importance used in summary writing, is *textual importance*. Items of textual importance are important to the author. A good reader can judge textual importance by looking at the structure of a text. For example, ideas that are mentioned repeatedly are almost always of textual importance. Authors can also clue us in to items of textual importance by the use of text features such as subheadings and main idea statements.

But there is another way of judging importance—*contextual importance*. Ideas of contextual importance relate to the personal experience and background of the reader. We've all encountered those little bits of text that somehow connect with us personally. Even though these ideas may not be of great importance to the author, readers still find them important (van Dijk and Kintsch 1978). Have you ever read an entire text with a group of students, only to have them fixate on one tiny detail? These students are focusing on contextual importance.

Students have trouble judging textual importance, and their summaries reflect this fact. The example summary is what happens when a student with little understanding of textual importance writes a summary. A teacher's attempts to correct this student may backfire. After all, the student did include the ideas that were important—to him. Recognizing that students may not understand textual importance is a crucial step toward helping them write better summaries.

Summary with Details of Contextual Importance

When people cut down trees and build houses plants are destroyed. There used to be lots of plants behind my house but they were all cut down. Put some plants in your garden so that the butterflies have a place to live.

Rule 2: Delete Trivia

This rule is often at odds with the rule about important information. To a student judging importance based on personal experiences, the line between trivia and important ideas is often hard to find. Also, the trivial ideas in a text are sometimes the most interesting.

In a study of eighth graders, Winograd (1984) found that poor readers who encountered a text about cities of the 1800s often included the same trivial details in their summaries. These details contained the interesting bits about rats, insects, catastrophic fires, and throwing garbage out of windows. Although these facts were not central to the main idea, there was something about them that attracted the attention of the readers.

Melissa's summary (Figure 3–2) includes trivial information. She ends her summary with the detail, "Monarch butterflys spread nectar to other plants." This information is not related to the main idea of the article. However, our class had visited our school butterfly garden several days before we completed the activity, and we had observed several monarch butterflies. Melissa probably included this information because it had personal importance to her.

As with the rule about including important ideas, teaching students to look for ideas of contextual importance—what's important to the author—is the key to helping them weed out the trivia from their summaries.

Directions: In the space below, write a
summary of the article. Remember to use
the subheadings to help you figure out
important ideas.

A lot of plants grow
in the area. They need
raid to survive. Some
plants are disapperaing
because of the shops
and houses that are
being built. The plants
need sun, water and
soil. But they don't
need as much if they
are growing well.
Some times monarch
Butterflys spread
nectar to other plants.
They help them.

FIGURE 3–2. Melissa's Summary

Rule 3: Delete Repeated Information

When authors develop an idea, they sometimes repeat information to make the point more clear. Repeated information should be deleted from summaries.

Studies show that the deletion rules are the first to develop. Even very young readers can delete ideas from a text to form a summary. This is the famous "copy-and-delete" method, in which a reader moves sentence by sentence through the text, choosing which sentences to take out and which to copy almost verbatim into the summary (Hidi and Anderson 1986). Ideas are not combined or condensed, and these summaries never show information integrated across paragraphs.

When texts follow a cohesive pattern, like the native plants article, students can use this strategy with some success. Many learn that copying the first sentence of each paragraph will usually work. The problem? The copy-and-delete strategy isn't a stopping point on the way to better summary writing, but an obstacle in the road. As long as students have a reasonably functional strategy, one that works at least some of the time, they won't feel any great need to learn how to use the more complex rules that lead to increased comprehension (Brown and Day 1983).

The following example summary shows the copy-and-delete strategy in action. Many of the sentences are taken directly from the text. A teacher pressed to cover a curriculum in a limited number of days may be tempted just to let the copy-and-delete summary slide—after all, the student produced something that resembles a summary.

When allowed, some students will take the copy-and-delete strategy all the way through high school and into college. This is a problem! Fortunately, teaching students techniques for paraphrasing can help them to use the deletion strategy more effectively.

Summary Using the Copy-and-Delete Method

Native plants are the plants that naturally grow in an area. Orchids, sawgrass, and leather ferns grow in Florida. But native plants are disappearing. Native plants are great to grow. When you choose native plants, think about the amount of sun the plant needs. Some plants can't stand to have their roots wet. Pay attention to the eventual size of the plant.

Rule 4: Collapse Lists

After students have mastered deletion strategies, the rule of collapsing lists often develops next. Texts often contain lists of events or items. When students are faced with these lists of items or events in a text, they have several choices. They can delete the entire idea, repeat it exactly, use an efficient overall term, or use an inefficient overall term.

Suppose a text discusses items found in Egyptian tombs—precious oil, gold, gems, and ivory. A student using the copy-and-delete strategy would either copy this list or get rid of it entirely. A student developing the more sophisticated collapsing lists strategy could choose an inefficient category name for these items, like *jewels*. Gold and gems could be called jewels, but precious oil and ivory definitely do not fit this category. Finally, a student who is able to collapse the list with ease could group all the items together under the heading *valuables*.

When can students begin to do this? In studies, fifth graders were reluctant to leave the comfort zone of the copy-and-delete method. By seventh grade, some students were using inefficient overall terms, and by tenth grade, most were able to collapse lists with ease (Brown and Day 1983).

In the following summary, the ideas sunlight, moisture, and size have been collapsed into the general term *the plant's needs*.

Summary with a Collapsed List

Native plants are the plants that naturally grow in an area. They are important because the animals of an area depend on them. But they are disappearing. If you grow native plants in your garden, think about *the plant's needs*.

Rule 5: Choose or Create a Topic Sentence

This rule is the heart of summary writing. Students need to be able to identify the most important ideas in a text and restate those ideas in their own words.

Intermediate students are usually reluctant to combine ideas within and across paragraphs. This is another symptom of the sentence-by-sentence, copy-and-delete strategy. Novice readers stick to making meaning at the sentence level; skilled readers know that the meaning of a text is a global understanding of the entire text. A well-developed summary should integrate the ideas in the text and show this global understanding.

This rule presents several problems for students. We know that poor readers are not always sensitive to what adults would deem important in a text, and so they do not choose appropriate topic sentences (Winograd 1984). Even when students are aware of what is important, they rarely create new topic sentences, even at the college level (Brown and Day 1983).

The following example summary shows ideas from Figure 3–1, paragraph 4, combined in a sentence with ideas from paragraph 1. This is an example of how a student can create topic sentences in a summary.

Summary with a Created Topic Sentence

Although native plants are beautiful and important to wildlife, they are disappearing. *People can easily grow native plants in their gardens because they are accustomed to the conditions of an area.* When choosing a native plant, think about the plant's needs. Be sure that you have the right amount of sunlight, moisture, and space.

Chapter Summary

- Researchers have identified five rules for writing good summaries: Include important ideas, delete trivia, delete repeated ideas, collapse lists, and choose or create a topic sentence.

- The ability to use these rules to write a good summary is developmental, with some rules learned sooner than others.

- Students and adults don't always find the same ideas in a text important.

- When students don't know how to use the summarizing rules effectively, they may fall back on the copy-and-delete strategy, just copying certain parts of the text.

- "Collapsing a list" is creating a general title or category for a list of objects, ideas, or events.

- Selecting or creating a good topic sentence is an important element of summarizing.

Can we teach students how to follow these rules? Can we help them become better at summarizing and comprehending text? Of course we can! In the next part of the book, you will learn many classroom-tested strategies and activities for helping students to improve.

FINDING OUT WHAT STUDENTS ALREADY KNOW

4

The more I worked with summary writing, the more I realized that writing a good summary depends on a host of other skills. I decided to teach these skills explicitly in my classroom. Of course, just learning the individual skill was not the overall goal. I emphasized to students that they needed to be able to apply these skills to their reading and writing on an everyday basis. Summarizing wasn't just something we talked about for a day and then abandoned, but a strategy that I expected them to use in the next class, the next week, the next month.

Instead of just having students write summaries all year long, it's easy to teach skills that help students to summarize without writing a formal product. I like to incorporate an activity or lesson as I see that students need it. For example, while working on our research report unit, I saw that students needed to learn how to paraphrase. So I developed paraphrasing activities to help students take notes for their reports. The students had an instant reason to learn the skill and plenty of opportunity to practice on their own.

When students read fiction, we work with some of the strategies for narrative text. In the short story unit, for example, students worked with story sequence and collapsing lists. When we read dramas, we used universal themes to compare plays across cultures. Of course, summarizing can function quite well as part of a longer unit. When our reading curriculum was reorganized according to genre, I saw the nonfiction unit as a great place to focus on summarizing. I assessed the students using some of the checklists and reading selections you will find later in this chapter, and then used each skill as a small group lesson. The groups worked on the same skills, but with different texts chosen according to their reading levels.

As I planned lessons for teaching summarizing, I did not just want to photocopy workbook pages that everyone needed to do. My students all have different skills and abilities, and I need to differentiate my instruction to meet their needs best. But how could I find out what each student needed? First, I found out what they already knew about summarizing, then I made plans for how to teach them. Here is a glimpse into the process.

The First Step: Recognizing a Good Summary

I wanted students to be able to write a good summary. To assess their own work, they needed to be able to distinguish between a good summary and a bad one. Sounds easy, right?

A little research showed otherwise. The ability to tell a good summary from a bad one seems to develop somewhere around fourth grade. When presented with three different versions of a summary—a "bad" summary with interesting information, a "less good" summary with the copy-and-delete strategy, and a "good" summary representing all the rules from Chapter 3—students in second grade preferred the "bad" summary with the interesting information to the other two. Fourth and sixth graders were able to reject the "bad" summary, but some still preferred the longer, less coherent "less good" one (Hahn and Garner 1985). This shows that students need to see summaries of differing quality so that they can become more sensitive to the criteria.

See what your students think. After reading the article "Gardening with Native Plants" from the Chapter 3, present students with the "Native Plant Summaries" page (Figure 4–1). This figure shows three summaries of varying quality. Summary 1 includes some random details from throughout the article, whereas the third summary includes many personal opinions and ideas. Only summary 2 is a good example. Are your students drawn to summaries that highlight interesting information over important ideas? If so, your summary instruction should begin with how to recognize important information.

As I move on with summary writing, I continue to show students examples of different summaries for us to discuss. Sometimes I will put student work on the overhead; sometimes I will retype a few summaries and give everyone a copy. (I am always careful to ask a student's permission before I put her work in front of the class.) The discussion that develops is always interesting. Like the students in the study I discussed earlier, many of my pupils have come to equate a long piece of writing with a good one. Summaries do not necessarily follow this formula!

Native Plant Summaries

Which summary is best?

#1

Native plants are the plants that naturally grow in an area. Orchids, sawgrass, and leather ferns grow in Florida. But native plants are disappearing. Native plants are great to grow. When you choose native plants, think about the amount of sun the plant needs. Some plants can't stand to have their roots wet. Pay attention to the eventual size of the plant.

#2

Although native plants are beautiful and important to wildlife, they are disappearing. People can easily grow native plants in their gardens because they are accustomed to the conditions of an area. When choosing a native plant, think about the plant's needs. Be sure that you have the right amount of sunlight, moisture, and space.

#3

Native plants are used to the rain in an area. They depend on the wildlife of an area for food and shelter. Native plants are being bulldozed over. That shouldn't happen! People need to protect native plants so that they don't become extinct. Put native plants in a forest. Have low-growing plants to attract bugs, reptiles, and amphibians. Have shrubs and understory trees for birds and squirrels.

Directions:

Choose which summary of "Gardening with Native Plants" is the best. Then, explain your choice on the lines below.

_____

_____

_____

_____

_____

_____

_____

FIGURE 4–1.

The Second Step: Summary Knowledge Rating

A knowledge rating is a simple checklist that students can use to rate their knowledge about a topic. Students read a column of ideas or terms and mark whether they have never heard of the topic, are somewhat familiar with the topic, or can explain it. An easy alternative to a pretest, knowledge ratings work well at the beginning of the year or a specific unit. Sometimes I ask a student to transcribe the data from individual knowledge ratings onto a poster, so that the whole class can see what is known and what needs to be studied.

I developed the Summary Writing Knowledge Rating (Figure 4–2) when I taught in middle school. Students came to our school from three different elementary schools, and I needed to find out what the students already knew about summarizing.

When I looked at the knowledge ratings my students turned in at the beginning of the year, I could quickly see that many students felt comfortable with summarizing and main ideas, had heard of paraphrasing and trivia, but were completely unfamiliar with collapsing lists and identifying text structure. Andrea's knowledge rating (Figure 4–3) is an example of a completed form.

Of course, a knowledge rating can't always be trusted. Sometimes I've had students check off that they know everything, even when they can't explain any of the terms. They seem to think that this will make them look smarter! Make sure that students know that this is a sort of pretest that won't be graded or judged. Also, collect the knowledge ratings and look at them yourself. A student may check off that he can explain "collapsing lists," but may offer an incomplete or incorrect explanation. This error can give you valuable information about what students are thinking, and can help you to design lessons to address any misconceptions.

After the class has completed the activity, students put the knowledge ratings in a portfolio. At the end of the unit, they can look back to their initial understandings and see what they have learned.

The Third Step: Reading Student Summaries

Rating summaries and completing knowledge ratings are good ways to find out what your students are thinking. However, sooner or later, you will have to actually *read* the summaries that your students produce.

Teachers are often reluctant to grade summaries. It's easy to understand why. Standard text response rubrics just don't work very well with

Summary Writing Knowledge Rating

Directions:

Rate your knowledge of each summarizing skill below. If you mark that you can explain the term, please do so!

Term	Never heard of it	Have seen/heard before	I can write an explanation
Summary			
Main idea			
Paraphrasing			
Trivia			
Collapsing lists			
Text structure			
Theme			

FIGURE 4–2.

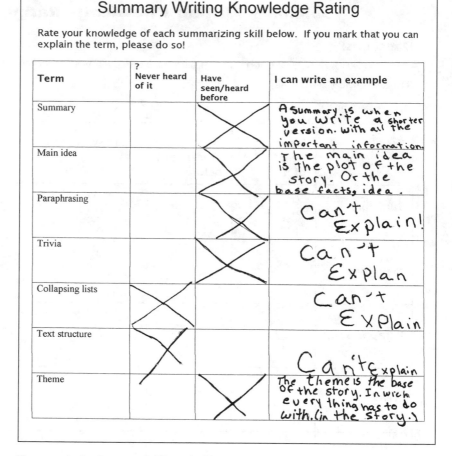

Summary Writing Knowledge Rating

Rate your knowledge of each summarizing skill below. If you mark that you can explain the term, please do so!

Term	? Never heard of it	Have seen/heard before	I can write an example
Summary		X	A Summary is when you write a shorter version. With all the important information.
Main idea		X	The main idea is the plot of the story. Or the base facts, idea.
Paraphrasing		X	Can't Explain!
Trivia		X	Can't Explain
Collapsing lists	X		Can't Explain
Text structure	X		Can't explain
Theme		X	The theme is the base of the story. In wich every thing has to do with. (in the story.)

FIGURE 4–3. Summary Knowledge Rating

a summary. The summary rubrics that are available are often skimpy. When I read them carefully, I could sometimes give a high score to what I knew was a substandard summary.

I decided to write my own assessment. The Summary Checklist is one that I designed to assess student summaries and guide my instruction (Figure 4–4). I don't use it for grading or day-to-day work—it's just too long. However, it is an excellent tool for occasional use. When paired with a classroom status chart, it can help you to create small groups of students for specific skill instruction.

In some ways, the list parallels the five rules for summarizing, but I did need to make some changes. Although paraphrasing is not specifically

Summary Checklist
Expository Text

Name _____   **Date** _____

Title of text _____

		Beginning	Developing	Proficient	Does not apply to text
Basic Summary Criteria	**Important ideas from the text**	Important ideas are missing OR Important ideas aren't stated accurately	Some important ideas are presented, but: • Some are missing • Used author's exact words • Doesn't use key vocabulary from the text	Important ideas are presented clearly and in the student's own words	
	Accurately paraphrases the author's words	Many inaccurate statements OR Copied directly from text	Attempt is made to paraphrase, but: • Awkward wording • Best words not chosen	The author's words are accurately and precisely paraphrased	
	Deletes trivia and repeated information	Many trivial or unimportant statements included	Some trivial or unimportant statements included	No trivial or unimportant statements included	
	Collapses lists	Lists are copied directly from text	Attempt is made to collapse list, but word choice is not accurate	Lists are collapsed with accurate terms	
	Reflects the structure of the text	Seems random OR Written in chronological order	Attempt is made to reflect structure of text	The structure of the text is apparent in the summary	
Optional Writing Criteria	**Word choice**	Words are not well-chosen, writing sounds awkward	Some specific words, may be slightly awkward or wordy	Brief and concise, specific, vivid words	
	Sentence variety	Sentences are short and choppy, with unintentional fragments or run-ons	Some attempt is made to include variety	Sentences have a variety of patterns, length, and beginning	
	Capitalization	Many errors in capitalization	Some errors in capitalization	Capitalization used where needed	
	Punctuation	Punctuation errors interfere with meaning	Punctuation choices are mostly correct	Punctuation choices are correct and enhance the writing	

FIGURE 4–4.

mentioned in the rules for summary writing, I did want to see whether students were able to do this. I added the criterion "Reflects the structure of the text" when I noticed some of my students writing every summary as if it were in chronological order—first, second, third, and so forth.

I included a separate section for conventions and style. As long as I am sitting down with a class set of summaries to read, I might as well assess some writing goals at the same time. If you are just working with summarizing as a reading skill, you may not want to take the time to assess punctuation, word choice, and brevity. You may also wish to eliminate this part if you are working with students who have writing difficulties.

Choosing the appropriate text for a baseline summary assessment is very important. Not just any nonfiction article will do. I wanted a fairly short selection that would require students to find a main idea, collapse a list, and have the opportunity to combine ideas across paragraphs. I also wanted to avoid a busy text with photographs, captions, and artwork, because these text features can distract students from a reading task.

When I had trouble finding the perfect text, I decided to write my own, "The American Chestnut" (Figure 4–5). The text is organized in problem-and-solution format. The first paragraph explains the historical significance of the chestnut, the second paragraph describes their demise, and the third paragraph offers a possible solution. I also included a word defined in context (blight) and, in the first paragraph, an opportunity to collapse a list.

After students read the text, I asked them to write a summary. I did not give any specific instructions about what a summary was, nor did I give them a length requirement. I allowed them to take as much time as they wanted. The entire process took less than thirty minutes of class time.

As I read the summaries, I kept track of whether they were including the important ideas from the text. I made a quick checklist for myself to help keep track. Notice that I only jotted down quick notes. I didn't take the time to explain each idea fully, because each student uses slightly different wording. If you are assessing student summaries for a different text, you may want to just underline words or phrases that you find important.

> *American chestnut*
>
> *dominant tree*
>
> *food for wildlife*
>
> *many uses*

The American Chestnut

Directions:

Read the text below. Write a summary on a separate sheet of paper.

The American chestnut once dominated the forests of the eastern United States. Growing up to 100 feet tall, it towered over the other trees in the forest. The abundant chestnuts that appeared every fall were important food sources for many animals, including wild turkeys, deer, and the now extinct passenger pigeon. Settlers used the wood of the chestnut tree for everything from fence posts to cradles to musical instruments.

But these trees are very rare today. A blight, or fungus, killed most of the American chestnut trees. This blight first appeared in 1904 and rapidly spread along the East Coast. People were horrified as their beloved trees sickened and died. By 1950, only a few were left. It seemed as if the American chestnut was gone forever.

But the story doesn't end there. A group of scientists wanted to bring back this beautiful and important tree. They knew that the Chinese chestnut, a low-growing shrub, did not get the blight. They worked to mix the Chinese chestnut with the American chestnut to create a kind of American chestnut that could withstand the blight. If their plans are successful, they will eventually begin replanting American chestnuts in forests, yards, and cities. Perhaps future generations will be able to enjoy the American chestnut once more.

FIGURE 4–5.

blight/fungus

few are left

scientists

mix with Chinese chestnut

replant trees

hope for future

Here are some examples of student summaries, along with notes about instruction.

Sean's summary (Figure 4–6) includes a great note at the bottom. "I don't know what a sumery is so I just rout the inportent stof." Even though I know that previous teachers have taught what a summary is, I'm used to many students being uncertain of what to do with this task. I always enjoy seeing how students try to do their best even through uncertainty.

Sean included three of nine main ideas in thirty words. He starts out with the important ideas from the first paragraph, but then his attention wandered or he became frustrated with the task. Deleting trivia was not a problem—in fact, he deleted so much that his summary does not reflect the problem and solution presented in the text.

With Sean, I began instruction with finding main ideas in the text. We next moved into examining text structure.

Jeremy's summary (Figure 4–7) reflects a slightly more sophisticated understanding of the summarizing task. Jeremy included five of nine main

The American chestnut grow in the united states. It grow up to 100 feet tall. In the fall it was a important food source. These trees are vary rare today.

I dont know what a sumery is so I just rout the inportent stof.

FIGURE 4–6. Sean's Summary

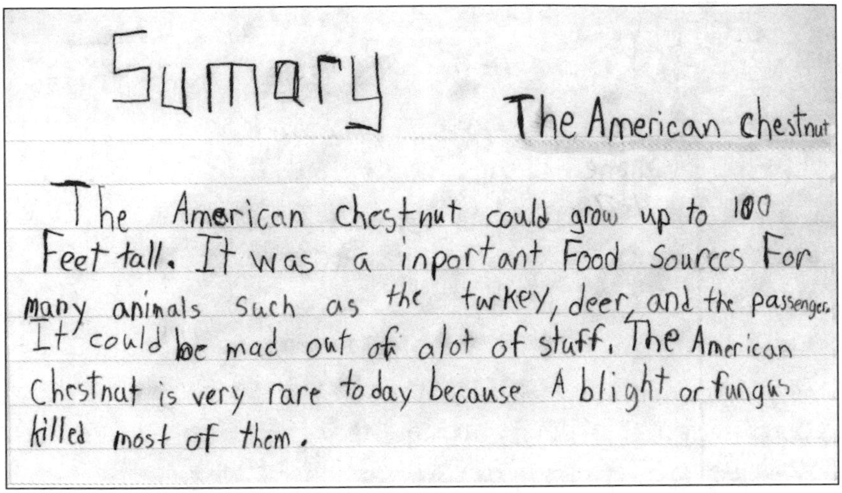

FIGURE 4–7. Jeremy's Summary

ideas in fifty-three words. Although he found the problem in the text, he omitted all the information that was included in the final paragraph. Jeremy needed to begin by working with text structure. Once he understood how an author crafts a piece of text, he did a better job of finding all the important ideas.

Jeremy could use some work in paraphrasing, because some of his phrases stray from the original meaning of the text. For example, he says that the chestnut "could be mad out of alot of stuff," when in fact it should be the other way around. Jeremy is also struggling with collapsing lists. Instead of listing the three different animals, he could have collapsed the list as "wildlife."

Andrea includes all the key ideas from the article in 122 words (Figure 4–8). She seems to have a good understanding of how to find main ideas, and her summary reflects the structure of the text.

But Andrea's summary can definitely be improved. Like Jeremy, she needs help with collapsing lists. Not only does she list all the examples of wildlife, but she also lists "yards, parks, towns, and cities," a list that could easily be collapsed to "places."

Andrea was making attempts to paraphrase. Did you notice the way she described the height of the chestnut—"at a extent of 100 ft"? This is a new way of stating the author's idea. In other places, though, she seemed to copy the words of the author, as with the sentence about the settlers. Andrea is ready for more instruction in paraphrasing.

The American Chestnut

The American chestnut once grew rappidly in the Forests. It towered over every other kind of tree, at a extent of 100 ft. These trees provided food for wild turkeys, the extinct passenger pigeon, & deer. Settlers used it's wood to make anything from fence posts to cradles. But, now the American Chestnut is rare. A fungus killed most of this beautiful tree. The Chinese Chestnut, a low growing shrub, could not get the fungus. A group of scientists wanted to bring the American Chestnut. So they worked to mix the Chinese & American Chestnut, to creat a Chestnut that could withstand the fungus. They will eventually plant them in yards, parks, towns, & cities. So we can enjoy the beautiful Chestnut again.

FIGURE 4–8. Andrea's Summary

Brittney's summary is as interesting. She is an artistic, intuitive student who does not think in a linear way, and her summary (Figure 4–9) reflects this. With five of nine important ideas in seventy-six words, her statistics resemble Jeremy's. Unlike Jeremy, however, she scatters information from differerent paragraphs throughout her summary. For instance, she

> This was about a Chesnut tree and it is very, very big. A type of fungus started to spread around. These trees have becom very rare. This Chesnut tree is special because they are rare and towers 100 ft in the Air. 1950 is when the noticed that only a few Chesnut trees are still livieing. If there plans are succseccful the will eventually start planting more chesnut tree in the forest, cities, and also yard.

FIGURE 4–9. Brittney's Summary

mentions the blight before she describes the size of the trees. I'm curious about why she is doing this, and want to include her in text structure instruction. She seems to be processing the text in an unusual way.

Next Steps

To help me plan my small groups, I made a simple class status chart. I simply wrote the skills that I planned to teach at the top of the paper, and then jotted down student names under each heading as I saw their needs.

You will probably see a great deal of overlap in the student groups. I certainly did! A student who has trouble finding main ideas is unlikely to be an expert at collapsing lists. I decided to start with the most basic skills. For instance, Sean would benefit most by starting off with finding main ideas. This isn't to say that he wouldn't learn from a lesson on paraphrasing or text structure. However, work with main ideas would probably produce the most improvement in the least amount of time.

Perhaps you notice that *all* your students need a particular skill. You can teach them all at once or you can weave instruction in that skill into your regular reading groups. Last year, I needed to make sure that all my students were proficient with finding main ideas. So I worked with main ideas with each one of my reading groups, altering the texts to allow for their different reading levels.

However you plan your instruction, be sure to keep copies of the students' first summaries, knowledge ratings, and checklists. You will find that they are great tools for communicating with parents and other staff members.

Chapter Summary

- Before teaching about a subject, it's important to find out what students already know.

- By looking at how students rate summaries, a teacher can learn whether students know how to spot a good summary.

- A summary knowledge rating can show what students have already learned about summarizing.

- Assessing student summaries with a checklist gives insight into what aspects of a summary a student can do well, and what a student needs to improve.

In the next part of the book, you will find specific chapters relating to each of the smaller skills for summary writing. Each chapter includes a discussion of the skill as well as whole group activities, small group activities, and considerations for standardized tests.

TOPICS AND MAIN IDEAS

5

As I jumped into summary writing with my seventh graders, I expected to focus on the finer points of paraphrasing, condensing, and wording. I quickly changed my thinking.

"Cody, a main idea is best expressed in a sentence. Here, you say that 'Giant squid is the main idea of this article.' That's not the main idea," I said patiently.

"Oh." Cody, chewing on his pencil, studied his paper for a moment. Then his face lit up in an excited smile. "Oh, I see! I'll go fix it," he said, and happily walked away while I basked in the glow of my good teaching.

Two minutes later, he returned to my side. His corrected answer read, "The main idea of this article is the giant squid."

My students were having terrible difficulties with finding the main ideas in articles. These difficulties translated into their writing as well. "This paragraph is about my animal's habitat," read one student's report. I soon realized that I would have to leave the finer points of summary writing for the future. Right now, my students needed to learn the difference between topics and main ideas.

What's the Difference?

To many people, *topic* is the same as *main idea*. The two are related, but are definitely not the same. Although there has been some academic debate about the difference, the most widely agreed-upon definition states that a topic is the superordinate word or phrase to which all the ideas in a passage refer. The topic of a reading can usually be stated in one or two words. It's the general subject of a reading. For instance, what do kids like to read about? Dinosaurs. Skateboarding. Disasters. Aliens. These are all topics (Aulls 1975).

The main idea of a text is usually stated in a sentence or two. The main idea is the statement that the author makes about the topic, or the most important idea in the text (Sjostrom and Hare 1984). Most expository texts contain a hierarchy of ideas, with an overall main idea supported by chapter, section, and paragraph main ideas. (Different expository text structures are discussed in Chapter 6.) A book with the topic dinosaurs, for example, may have the main idea, "Dinosaurs were amazing in their complexity and variety." The book might develop this main idea by describing the adaptations of dinosaurs and the many different species that existed. A book about skateboarding may express the main idea, "Skateboarders overcome challenges through practice and effort," and develop that main idea with chapters about how skateboarders develop their skills. Topics, then, are usually one- or two-word phrases, whereas main ideas are expressed in sentences.

Finding Topics in Text

Usually the topic of a text will be apparent by looking at the title, pictures, or subheadings. In Cody's giant squid article, the topic was repeated in the title, the first paragraph, and numerous photos.

Higher level text may confuse students by dancing around the topic instead of stating it directly. In these cases, teach students to look for repeated references to help them find a topic. If an idea is referred to over and over again, it's probably important. Sometimes, students don't recognize repeated references because an author uses different words. Look at the following paragraph. The same idea (pothole wetlands) is repeated four times in the paragraph, but is referred to in different ways.

> You may have a wetland at your house and not even know it. Sometimes, *small depressions* in the lawn fill up with rain and hold the moisture for days at a time. These "*potholes*" often come alive at night with creatures like spring peepers (tiny frogs), insects, and birds. When people avoid these wet *areas* and don't mow *them*, they are providing a habitat for animals—without even knowing it!

Suggestions for Teaching Students How to Find Topics in Text

Your school library is an excellent place to introduce students to topics in text. If the library is arranged by the Dewey Decimal System, the books are organized according to their topics. There are a number of different activities that you can use to explore Dewey topics with your students.

Category Scramble, Version 1.　　Take a library cart and gather fifteen to twenty books on about five different topics. (Better yet, ask a librarian or aide to pull the books for you!) In the classroom, scramble the books and ask a group of students to sort them according to their topics. Once the sorting is done, discuss the process that the students used. How did they know which books went together? What clues helped them out?

Category Scramble, Version 2.　　Students who are adept at version 1 can build on their understandings of topics with this adaptation. As before, pull fifteen to twenty books. This time, however, make the topics be somewhat similar. For example, include books about birds and books about reptiles, so that students will need to change from the broad topic of Animals to narrower topics like Birds and Reptiles. As before, talk about why students chose to categorize the books in the manner they chose.

Trouble with Main Ideas

Left to their own devices, most students write the topic of a text when they are asked to write a main idea. This hinders their comprehension. If students read only for topics, they are missing the ideas. As you will see later, two pieces of text can have the same topic but very different main ideas.

Teaching students to find main ideas is an ongoing process. Research shows that age may be a factor. Fourth and fifth graders (and probably middle school students who read below grade level) seem to connect ideas in a sentence only with those ideas that come immediately before or immediately after. When students concentrate so intently on individual sentences, they can rarely see the big picture, and following an author's argument is difficult (Kintsch 1990).

In Chapter 3, we saw that students don't always agree with adults about the important ideas of a passage. Children usually focus on what is exciting and unusual instead of significant. As I continued to work with Cody on the giant squid article, he had trouble understanding that the article was mostly about how the scientists gathered information about the creatures. Instead, he wanted to write about the gross pictures of dead squid!

The ability to find main ideas also depends heavily on the text. As you have probably experienced, students who can find main ideas in short, simple passages may fall down flat when it comes to longer passages.

Although numerous books of worksheets will claim that page after page of practice will teach students to find main ideas, in reality, it's not that simple. The text in controlled worksheets is much different from the text in real articles and books. The way that an author expresses a main idea can have a major impact on whether readers can find it.

Explicit Main Ideas

An explicit main idea is one that is stated directly by the author. These texts usually have a topic sentence that states the main idea, and then detail sentences to develop that thought. (This is the classic paragraph structure that we teach our students during writing time.) In the following paragraph, the topic is "wetlands," and the main idea is stated in the topic sentence. The remaining sentences serve as examples to show the reader how the wetlands are important in nature.

> Wetlands are very important in nature. For example, wet areas serve as "nurseries" for creatures of many species to raise their young. Wetlands also help to control flooding, and can filter out dangerous pollutants. When wetlands are drained or developed, the entire food chain suffers.

Explicit main idea paragraphs are all around us—and for good reason. Studies show that the best comprehension occurs in a paragraph with a clear topic sentence at the beginning of a paragraph (Davey and Miller 1990). If you browse through your students' social studies or science textbooks, you can probably find many examples of these kinds of paragraphs.

Sometimes, texts written in logical order and with a topic sentence at the beginning still confuse students. Suppose that the topic sentence were replaced with, "Wetlands serve many functions." Because this idea is more abstract, some students won't recognize it as the main idea of the paragraph. They may not recognize how the verb *serve* is used in this sentence, and will dump the information as being unimportant. Topic sentences with forms of *to be* and action verbs are easier for students to understand than topic sentences with the same information and a more abstract verb. Also, topic sentences written in the passive voice can also confuse students (for example, "Many functions are served by wetlands.").

> Wetlands serve many functions. Different kinds of creatures use these places to raise their young. Flooding can also be

absorbed and controlled by the marshy ground. Dangerous pollutants can be filtered out by wetland mud. Draining of wetlands causes problems in the entire food chain.

Most main idea workbooks are filled with paragraphs stating an explicit main idea. It is true that students should begin with these kinds of texts to find main ideas. However, if these easiest examples are all that students see, finding the main idea will become a simple exercise of just pointing to the first sentence.

But this strategy doesn't always work. Authors will occasionally put an explicit topic sentence at the end of a paragraph. In this case, the details lead up to the main idea. This is a pattern that can often be found in persuasive text, as writers build their case for an opinion or an idea.

Interestingly, readers process this kind of text differently from text with an explicit main idea as the first sentence. When a first sentence is not stated in general terms, proficient readers make guesses about possible main ideas and check these guesses against future sentences in the paragraph. This process takes a little longer and requires some additional thought for strong readers. Poor readers, though, may not even make and test these guesses. Instead, they tend to fall back on the first sentence as the main idea (Davey and Miller 1990). Think about how this will alter their comprehension! In the following paragraph, a reader who accepts the first sentence as the main idea would think that the paragraph was mostly about the insects of wetlands, instead of about the unpleasant aspects of wetland areas.

> Wetlands of all kinds often harbor annoying insects like mosquitoes and gnats. The constant wetness causes microorganisms to grow, which gives the area a lingering stench. The vegetation is usually thick and menacing, inhabited by many unusual creatures. For these reasons, wetlands have often been considered to be nasty, unpleasant places.

Standardized Tests and Explicit Main Ideas

Standardized tests often contain questions about main ideas. Sometimes students are faced with only a paragraph to read, whereas sometimes they must read and answer questions about a longer selection.

Standardized test preparation can be silent drudgery. I like using every-pupil-response (EPR) strategies to liven things up. EPR is a teaching strategy that accomplishes two purposes. Not only does it actively engage all the students, it also gives the teacher a way to look around the room and assess quickly how the class is doing. After hearing a question or challenge, every student responds by using hand signals like thumbs-up, thumbs-down, response cards, or movement.

To use EPR for standardized test preparation, begin by gathering a number of paragraphs from your state's standardized test resources, content area textbooks, or main idea workbooks. Put each paragraph on a transparency, along with three to five possible main ideas. Be sure to include the topic as one of the choices.

Next, hand out four notecards to each student. Tell them to label the first one a, then b, and so forth. Display the paragraphs and choices one at a time on the overhead projector, and have students hold up the card that corresponds to their answers. By looking around the room, you can quickly tell how students are doing with finding the main ideas of different kinds of paragraphs.

Suggestions for Teaching Topic and Main Idea

How do we help students who construct meaning sentence by sentence to look for the big picture? Falling back on workbooks and commercially prepared materials is not the answer. Students need to look at many different kinds of text to make the transfer between finding topics and main ideas as a school activity, to be done only when a teacher tells you to, and a real-life skill, to be used every time they read.

More on Teaching Topics and Main Ideas

As I excavated our school's book room, I found ancient reading workbooks in huge piles. One of the pages was actually called "Topic and Main Idea" and had several paragraphs about Mongolia. Students would read the different paragraphs and see that selections with the same topic can have different main ideas.

I wasn't about to hand out the moldy workbooks to my students, but the page helped me to create my own activity for assisting students to find topics and main ideas. We were studying electricity at the time, so I decided to create a topic and main idea page (see Figure 5–1) about the fascinating but little-known scientist Nikola Tesla.

Figure 5–1 may look like a worksheet that you can just assign to students to do on their own, and you are welcome to do this; however, I've

Topic and Main Idea

The topic of a piece of text can usually be stated in one or two words. The topic tells what the text is mostly about.

The main idea of a piece of text can usually be stated in a sentence. The main idea includes the topic and a main point about the topic.

Sometimes, pieces of text can have similar topics, but different main ideas.

Paragraph A

Nikola Tesla was born in a part of Europe called Serbia in 1856. Even in his early years, he showed a talent for science. As a child, Tesla loved to experiment and once made a flying aircraft powered by insects! While he studied at the university, he argued with his professors about electricity and how it could be generated and transmitted. Tesla traveled to America as a young man, arriving in New York with nothing but a few cents and some scraps of poetry in his pocket. He was quickly hired by Thomas Edison.

Paragraph B

Students should learn about Nikola Tesla. Everyone talks about Thomas Edison, but Tesla's accomplishments were greater. Edison fought bitterly with Tesla and tried to make people think that he was crazy. But it was Tesla's understanding of alternating current that made it possible to send electricity to large numbers of people. Tesla also discovered the radio (even though he didn't get the credit for it), and Tesla coils are still used today in televisions. Rumor has it that Tesla also invented an earthquake machine, experimented with a "death ray," and may even have contacted aliens. Tesla definitely deserves to be studied.

1. What is the topic of both paragraphs? _____

2. Choose one of the paragraphs to study more closely. (Circle one) A   B

3. Reread the paragraph to yourself. Underline the sentence that you think states the main idea.

4. Read the paragraphs with your partner. Share the main ideas you chose. Did you agree? Write a sentence to explain your choices.

_____

_____

_____

Figure 5–1.

© 2006 by Emily Kissner from *Summarizing, Paraphrasing, and Retelling*. Portsmouth, NH: Heinemann.

had the best success by using this as part of a small group activity. Before we begin, we talk about the difference between topics and main ideas, and why it is important to be able to find both in our reading. Then I give the students a few moments to scan the paragraphs silently and discuss any words they don't know. (They are usually very surprised that Nikola is a man's name!) Next, I pair students to read the paragraphs aloud to one another and answer the questions at the bottom. I keep the students at the small group area while they do this, so that I can hear their reading and their problem solving. This gives me an idea of the direction to take with their group in the future.

Watch the students as they underline (step 3 in Figure 5–1). If a pair starts randomly underlining groups of words in the paragraph, you know that their understanding of main idea is shaky at best. After the students are mostly finished, discuss their responses with the whole group. The topic of both texts is "Nikola Tesla" or "Nikola Tesla's achievements." Discuss how they could use repeated references to figure this out.

I've found that sixth graders are predictable—most choose to study paragraph A, and most can see that the first sentence, "Nikola Tesla was born in a part of Europe called Serbia in 1856," is not the main idea. Talk about how all the rest of the sentences support the idea of Tesla's talent for science in his early years. To the students, college age may not seem like "early years"—if this issue comes up, encourage the discussion.

As you discuss paragraph B, students may disagree on whether the first or the last sentence states the main idea. Talk about the similarities between the sentences. How would the paragraph be different if you took one of them out?

Finally, because the purpose of reading is to gather information, we end our discussion by talking about any new or interesting information they found. Students are intrigued by the earthquake machine and often want to know more. I encourage them to find answers to their questions by using resources like the Internet, books, or encyclopedia.

Create your own topic and main idea activities by choosing books or passages with similar topics and ask students to look for the differences in main ideas. This can carry over into a discussion of the author's purpose, as students compare informational texts and persuasive texts about the same topic.

To build students' understanding of explicit main ideas, use many short, simple texts. I've had the most success with the following order:

- Single paragraphs with explicit main idea at the beginning

- Single paragraphs with explicit main idea in another location

- Multiparagraph pieces with an explicit main idea

- Poorly written pieces

It's important to include instruction with poorly written pieces. Students will encounter a great deal of bad writing throughout their school careers! When you teach with bad writing, you can clearly show the relationship between writing and reading. As authors, students want their readers to be able to find the main ideas of what they write. If they do not make these ideas clear, readers will be frustrated.

Implicit Main Ideas

In the previous section, we explored the ways that authors can use topics and explicit main ideas to help their readers make meaning of the text. But, as always, there's a complication! Authors do not always state their ideas directly. Sometimes the main idea of a passage is *implicit*, or implied. This requires students to take an extra step with their thinking and put the details of a passage together into a main idea.

Why do authors do this? We know that many fourth and fifth grade readers are still making meaning at the local level, looking for connections between individual sentences instead of trying to make sense of a whole text. Even college students have been shown to have trouble inventing main idea statements when none are given. It seems as if everything would be easier if authors just made their ideas clear from the outset.

However, there are situations in which authors want to leave their main ideas implicit. Sophisticated adult readers usually prefer being able to come to their own conclusions, and dislike being hit over the head with a big idea at the start of every paragraph. Sometimes authors try to build interest and suspense by holding back and not revealing all their secrets. In essays and other conversational forms of writing, authors often take a chatty tone, and meander through paragraphs of commentary. In advertisements, companies hide an implicit main idea to try to persuade readers to buy a product or hold an opinion.

Let's consider a typical paragraph in which the main idea is implicit. Read the following paragraph and try to invent a main idea statement.

Forest wetlands occur in wet areas that can still support tall trees. Bogs, special wetlands that are found in the far north, contain an amazing array of strange plants. Seabeds and stream bottoms are also sometimes considered wetland habitats, as are sandy shores and tidal flats.

Hopefully, you came up with something along the lines of, "There are many different kinds of wetlands." Most readers begin by noticing that the word *wetland* appears several times, which means that it is probably the topic. Next, readers look at the sentences to see what the author is saying about wetlands. In this case, six different types of wetlands are mentioned, but only briefly described, which shows that the author is trying to make the point that there are many different kinds of wetlands.

Remember, when proficient readers don't encounter an explicit main idea in the first sentence, they form a guess about the main idea of the passage and then check later sentences against this guess (Davey and Miller 1990). If no main idea sentence is found, the reader will create one. Less able readers, of course, will often skip this step, and will accept one of the sentences of the paragraph as a main idea—or just decide that the main idea isn't worth finding!

Standardized Tests and Implicit Main Ideas

Instruction in implicit main ideas is important for standardized test success. A common task for both reading and writing is to provide students with a paragraph that has no topic sentence, and then ask students to choose the best topic sentence. This activity requires an ability to choose a main idea sentence from a given list. Take a look at this paragraph:

_____These birds nest in holes, or cavities, in large dead trees. Many people take down dead trees on their properties, leaving the bluebird with no place to live. Also, nonnative species such as English sparrows have pushed the bluebird out of the few nesting sites they have left. English sparrows will even kill baby bluebirds. As if this weren't enough, the bluebird nests in wide, open wetlands, which are being turned into roads and developments.

Suppose that the choices for the topic sentence of this paragraph were:

a. The Eastern bluebird has many interesting nesting habits.

b. English sparrows are crowding the Eastern bluebird out of its home.

c. Eastern bluebirds and English sparrows do not get along.

d. The Eastern bluebird faces several problems.

All of the possibilities are congruent with the information in the paragraph. The fact that "English sparrow" is repeated twice in the paragraph may lead students to think that the main idea should include this bird. However, only answer d is the main idea supported by all the details.

Suggestions for Teaching Implicit Main Ideas

Implicit Main Ideas Student Page.   My sixth graders were not doing well with implicit main ideas. Tired of explaining the same thing over and over, I decided to make an implicit main ideas activity (Figure 5–2) suitable for the whole class.

Trying to get a challenging class of thirty twelve-year-olds all to do the same thing at the same time can be like playing the "Whack-A-Mole" game at a carnival—as soon as one group of students is focused and under control, another group will flare up. So I design my resources accordingly. When we worked on this, I had students clear their desks of everything else. I called on students to read the instructional details at the top of the page. I put all the information that students need to complete a task on the resource itself. This helps me in two ways. Students who were absent for the lesson can easily find the information they missed. And when administrators drop by to visit, I can hand them the resource sheet so they can instantly see my objectives.

I wanted to build in a partner activity, so I put directions on the resource sheet. Implicit main ideas are quite challenging. I did not want to overload students' working memories with new concepts and ideas, so I wrote a reading selection that would be fairly simple for them to understand. This way they could focus on the new skill, writing implicit main ideas.

The main idea of the paragraph on the left is that middle school is not as bad as students fear; the main idea of the one on the right is that staying organized is important. However, any main idea that is supported by all the details in the paragraph is acceptable. While students work on

Implicit Main Ideas Student Page

Sometimes the main idea of a passage is not stated. This is called an implicit, or implied, main idea. When you read this kind of passage, you need to figure out the main idea so that you can understand the author's main point.

Directions:

1. Read the paragraphs below. In the space provided, write a sentence to express the main idea of each paragraph.

Before you arrive in middle school, you will probably have an open house or orientation. This will be your chance to tour the school and meet the teachers. On the first day, there will be plenty of staff members in the halls to direct you to your homeroom. Teachers are always ready to help you open your lockers and answer your questions. Even the older students are not so bad. Many schools even have a buddy program that pairs older students with younger ones.

Be sure to start with an organized binder. Use folders or dividers to give each class its own section. Some teachers will want you to set up your notebook in a certain way, while others will let you decide. Don't wait to put papers in their proper places. At the end of each class, sort through your classwork and notes to get everything organized. When you have tests, quizzes, and homework, you will be able to find things more easily.

Main idea:

_____

_____

_____

Main idea:

_____

_____

_____

2. Share your main ideas with a partner. Think about the following questions:

   - Do your main idea statements agree?
   - What clues in each paragraph helped you to create a main idea statement?

FIGURE 5–2.

the sharing part of this activity, I circulate around the classroom to hear their conversations.

A classroom climate that supports risk taking is very important for these kinds of activities. If students feel that there is one and only one right answer, they will stop thinking creatively. Support and applaud their efforts to wrestle with ideas and put their thinking into words. Of course, this doesn't mean that you should accept every answer! Instead, praise purposeful and reflective thinking.

Here's an example of how I do this in my own classroom. After students have had an opportunity to share their main idea statements with a partner, I ask if anyone has changed their thinking as a result of the discussion. "As you worked with a partner, did anyone find that their initial main idea sentence needed to be changed? Could someone share their thinking?" A few students will volunteer, and will talk about how the sentence they wrote at first didn't work. I thank the students for sharing and praise the way that they changed their thinking.

Make up a Main Idea Activity. During this activity, students will get up and move as they try to form groups of related ideas. Once the students get together in topic groups, they will read their individual details and try to formulate a main idea.

How to do it:

1. Make topic cards by putting the following topics onto colored notecards.

   a. *Topics:* (one per notecard) Laura's binder, breakfast at Grandma's, the basketball team, cabin in the woods

2. Make detail cards by writing one detail on each white notecard.
   a. *Details:* (one per notecard) Pancakes are raw in the middle. Bacon is burned. Biscuits are hard like hockey pucks. Coffee is a light brown color. Milk has lumps. Oatmeal is stuck to the pan. Hog the basketball court at practice time. Laugh at other teams. Steal equipment from the equipment room. Don't keep score accurately. Show up late for games. Yell at the referees. Every paper is neatly clipped in. Reinforcements are color coded by subject. Writing utensils are in alphabetical order. Notes are neatly recopied each night. All materials are easy to find. Assignments are written on a homework list

at the end of each class. A brook gently flows nearby. Birds sing from the branches. The trees block the afternoon sun, making everything cool and pleasant. The pine trees tower above tall and fragrant. Everyone sits on the front porch and relaxes. Little glints of sunshine light up the ground.

3. Give each student a copy of the make up a main idea page (Figure 5–3). Give them time to read over the directions and ask any questions. *Teaching note:* Although it may be tempting to read directions aloud, build students' independence by having them read the directions themselves. Then allow time for students to ask questions and clarify the expectations. When setting up a group activity, it's always a good idea to make your behavior expectations clear. For this activity, you may want to give students a time limit and a silent signal so that you can get their attention quickly.

4   After students understand the activity, hand out the cards. This activity is set up for a maximum of twenty-nine students. If you have more than twenty-nine, add some additional details for each topic. For fewer students, take out a card or two from each page. Don't forget to hand out the topic cards!

5. After students have grouped themselves, remind them to work together to create a main idea. (If they are having trouble, advise them to think about their topic, plus a feeling or attitude about the topic.) Circulate as students work to hear their discussions, and challenge them to choose specific, vivid words in their main idea statements.

6. Finally, have the groups share their details and their main ideas. Reinforce the kind of thinking that students have been doing— looking at details and creating main ideas to go along with them.

Implicit Main Ideas in Writing

Teaching implicit main ideas works perfectly with instruction in report writing. When students take their notes, put them into categories, and write topic sentences, they are working with implicit main ideas.

If you keep getting reports that read, "This paragraph is about the description of the cardinal," your students need to work on implicit main

Make up a Main Idea

Sometimes authors don't state their main ideas directly. Main ideas that are not stated are called implied main ideas.

Directions:

Today, you will work with others in the class to think about lists of details and create your own main idea statements.

1. Read your card carefully. Think about whether it is a topic card or a detail card.

2. When your teacher gives the signal, get out of your seat and look for other students whose cards are similar to yours. If you have a detail card, try to match yourself with a topic. If you have a topic card, try to find your details.

3. Once you are in a group with a topic and several details, read your details aloud to one another. Try to figure out a main idea to go along with all of the details. (Hint: A main idea consists of a topic and a specific feeling or attitude about the topic.) Do **not** begin with "The main idea is …"

4. If time allows, develop a paragraph based upon your main idea and details.

My card says _____

_____

I think it is a (circle one)   **topic**   **detail**

> **Record the main idea your group creates**

Now write a paragraph using your group's details and main idea.

FIGURE 5–3.

ideas. They need to see that the details about the cardinal's appearance add up to a main idea.

When I teach this with students, I often put several supporting details on sentence strips and post them at the front of the room. Then, I hand out sentence strips to groups of students and give them a chance to try to compose their own topic sentences. Groups read their topic sentences aloud to the class and categorize them as "highly effective," "somewhat effective," and "not effective." (It's important to let the students categorize their own sentences before class discussion.) Class members can then tell whether they agree or disagree with the groups' ratings. Repeat this one or two times with different groups. As students gain experience in writing topic sentences, they will also gain the confidence they need to work independently.

Chapter Summary

To write a good summary, students need to be able to find topics and main ideas. Although topics can be expressed as a word or phrase, main ideas are usually best expressed in complete sentences. A main idea can be *explicit*, or stated by the author, or *implicit*, not directly stated by the author.

- Start by teaching students the difference between topics and main ideas.

- Work with texts that have explicit main ideas before introducing texts with implicit main ideas.

- Make the connection to writing class by having students use the strategy of writing implicit main ideas for writing topic sentences.

- In this chapter, we looked at how the choices made by an author at the paragraph level can affect a reader's comprehension. But authors make larger choices. How an entire text is crafted can have a major impact on how a reader understands the text. Being able to find the structure of a text is important for being able to write a good summary. In the next chapter, we look at how students understand text structure.

TEXT ORGANIZATION

6

Sometimes it's difficult to decide what is important for students to know, and what is not. As teachers, we know a great deal about how students read and make meaning of text. Do the students themselves need to know the names of the four reading stances? Do they need to know about Vygotsky's zone of proximal development? Do students need to know what to call different text structures?

This question came up as a colleague of mine prepared for a staff development workshop. A gifted reading and writing teacher, she had worked to create a session in which participants learned patterns of text organization by reading science picture books. The organizers of the workshop, however, were less than impressed. "Are you sure that students need to know text structures?" they asked, after seeing her plans. "Isn't that a little advanced for elementary and middle students?"

She argued her case, and fortunately prevailed. The teachers in the workshop responded enthusiastically. "This is just what we need!" one participant said. "This will be such a help in teaching nonfiction text."

Text organization is something that students of all ages can and should learn. In order for students to be able to summarize text, they need to understand that authors make conscious choices about how text is organized. In previous chapters, we saw that students have trouble differentiating between what is important to the author (textually important) and what is important to the reader (contextually important). Teaching students how to use the structure of the text to find the textually important information is a crucial step on the road to summarizing.

Novice readers are still making meaning at the microlevel, working sentence by sentence (Kintsch 1990). Many students ignore text features such as subheadings, or skip over cue words. Talking about text organization helps students to see the macrolevel, or overall structure, of the text, and gives them a framework to figure out how all the small pieces of information fit together. Little wonder that research shows that knowledge of text structure has a positive effect on comprehension. Students as young as second grade have been taught to identify text structures and use this knowledge to improve comprehension and questioning (Feldt, Feldt, and Kilburg 2002).

When you teach students how to use the organization of a text, you are equipping them with a powerful tool for reading, learning, and summarizing. Even better, text organization is not difficult to teach, and carries over into writing class as well.

But what does text organization really mean? Basically, it refers to both the internal structure of the writing and the physical layout of the text. Because the physical layout of the text is a more concrete and visual concept, I usually begin my instruction there.

What the Text Looks Like: Physical Layout

Have you ever put down a book because the text wasn't appealing, looked too dense, or just seemed boring? Readers make many judgments about a text simply based on the way that the writing is arranged on the page. Features such as captions, graphics, subheadings, and italicized print are merely surface features of the text, but they can enhance—or detract from—the author's message.

Adult readers know that the extra text on a page isn't just fluff to gloss over, but is important to comprehension. Many students, though, treat the subheadings and captions as a chore, and will skip them unless told otherwise! This affects not just their comprehension, but their ability to produce summaries as well. Suppose that someone told you to write a summary of the preceding chapter. You would probably refer back to the text organization and use the subheadings to help you decide what information is textually important. The subheading "Explicit Main Ideas," for example, would guide you to include information about the topic. The story about the giant squid article, however, does not have its own subheading. This might lead you to exclude those details from your summary. Using the text features can help a reader to decide quickly what is important and what is not. When students skip over text features, summary writing becomes more difficult.

Not all text features are equally important, however. I have found that most text features perform one of four functions. Titles, subheadings, and main idea statements all serve to *highlight main ideas*. Bold and italicized print, colored text, and pull quotes can all *show important details*. Graphs, photographs, and pictures can *explain* ideas to help a reader understand. And sidebars and captions both *add additional information*.

You may want to use these categories with your students, or you may want to create your own. Whichever you choose, show that there can be overlap between the text features and categories. Photographs, for example, often explain ideas in a visual way. However, sometimes a text will include a photograph that only marginally relates to the main idea of the text. In this case, the photograph would add additional information instead of explaining the ideas in the main portion of the text.

What about text features in fiction text? Most fiction, written to entertain, does not contain text features beyond pictures. Authors of fiction don't generally need to highlight main ideas or explain facts and concepts. Graphic novels, however, do use more text features to tell stories, and there are other fiction books that include lists and diagrams as well. Challenge students to find fiction with text features. Talk about why the author chose to include the features and how they impact the text.

Before you can work with students to use text features for summarizing, they need to understand what text features are and how to find them.

Suggestions for Teaching Students How to Find Text Features
Overhead Projector Overlays. This idea has appeared in many places. Find a student textbook page that includes a variety of different text features. Make an overhead transparency of the page and use sticky notes to cover up the different features. Then, remove them one by one, discussing the name of the text feature and its purpose. I like to have a chart with the categories: highlight main ideas, show important details, explain, and add additional information. As students name a text feature, we discuss the job it is performing in the text and add it to the chart.

Text Feature Magazine Article Activity. This activity is a natural next step from the overhead transparency overlay. I arrange the students in pairs or groups and distribute copies of children's nonfiction magazines. *Muse* is a big favorite of intermediate students. (Of course I don't have any class sets, but that's okay. Each group can read a different magazine.) Then students follow the directions on the Text Features in Magazine Articles resource (Figure 6–1) to preview the article, look for text features, and consider how the text features enhance the text. When students like Melissa use this activity, they focus on using text features to help them understand the text (Figure 6–2).

Text Features in Magazine Articles

_____ **Record information about your article.**

Title of magazine _____

Date _____

Article name _____

Author _____

_____ **Preview the article. Make a list of text features that you notice.**

_____ _____ _____

_____ _____ _____

_____ _____ _____

_____ **Complete the ratings below.**

_____ How much do you already know about the topic?

   Very little   Some   A great deal

_____ Are you interested in the topic?

   No   A little   Very interested

_____ **Read the article.** On another sheet of paper, write a summary of the article.

_____ Go back to the text features you found before you read. Think about the purpose of each feature.

Categorize the text features on the chart below.

(Some text features could go in more than one column.)

Text features that highlight **main ideas**	Text features that highlight **important details**	Text features that **explain**	Text features that **add information**

FIGURE 6–1.

Text Features

✓ Record information about your article.

Title of magazine Scolastic News   Date 9/16

Article name Interview with a Bully   Author Denise Rinaldo

✓ Preview the article. Make a list of text features that you notice.

captions   headings   preview
bold faced words   title   pronunciation
interduction   special fetures   predict

✓ Complete the ratings below.

How much do you already know about the topic?
Very little   (Some)   A great deal

Are you interested in the topic?
No   (A little)   Very interested

✓ **Read the article**. On another sheet of paper, write a summary of the article.

_____ Go back to the text features you found before you read. Think about the purpose of each feature. Categorize the text features on the chart below. (Some text features could go in more than one column.)

Text features that highlight *main ideas*	Text features that highlight *important details*	Text features that *explain*	Text features that *add information*
~~captions~~	bold words	pronuncitain	special fetures
headings	preview	interdution	headings
title	captions	captions	prouncitactions

FIGURE 6–2. Student Example of "Text Features in Magazine Articles"

Adding Features to Text. Books by Seymour Simon work wonderfully for this activity. Although his books contain beautiful photographs and well-written text, there are no text features to guide the reader along. Independently or in small groups, students have use sticky notes to add text features to a book. Have the groups present their altered versions to one another and talk about how the text features helped them or did not help them to understand the text.

Using Text Features to Predict. This is a generic activity that can be used with any nonfiction text. Create a three-column chart. Call one column Text Features, the second column Predictions, and the third column Reflections. Put text features from the article in the first column. Then, have students record predictions in the second column. For example, I used this chart before we read an article called "The Quick Little Fellows" from *Cricket* magazine. The title led students to predict that the article would be about people winning a race. However, the pictures in the article showed people sitting down and eating. They recorded their conflicting predictions and read the article, in which they learned that "quick little fellows" are actually chopsticks. Then, they recorded their reflections in the third column of the chart. This activity helps students to reflect on their thinking before and after reading.

Text Structure

The physical layout of a text is easy to see. To help students understand text organization, however, it is necessary to go one level deeper, to dive inside the actual text and examine its internal organization. This is text structure.

Needless to say, students usually find text structure more difficult than text features! But students need to be able to follow the author's pattern of organization. Students who don't understand that texts can be structured in different ways often end up writing summaries in a strange chronological order: "First the author talked about . . . *next* the author talked about . . . *then* the author talked about . . ." It's as if the students are writing about their experience with the text instead of the text itself.

Intermediate students are already somewhat familiar with the internal structure of fiction text. They know that they will meet characters who will work through a plot to resolve a conflict. Nonfiction text is organized quite differently, however, and that is what we will examine in the remainder of this chapter.

The original research on text structure identified five basic structures (Meyer 1985). They are

1. Description

2. Listing

3. Cause and effect

4. Comparison

5. Problem and solution

As I have worked with students, I have added two other text structures:

6. Main idea structure

7. Chronological order

Readers determine the structure of a text by looking for cue words and text features. An essay organized in compare-and-contrast order, for example, might include cue words such as *on the other hand* or *at the same time*. Chronological order text may include cue words such as *next* or *finally*.

As you work with text structure with students, remember that a text can have one overall structure and then use another structure for an individual paragraph. A chronological text about the Revolutionary War may include a paragraph to compare and contrast regular British soldiers and their Hessian counterparts. This is when an understanding of text features is helpful—often, authors will signal a departure from the overall text structure with a new subheading.

A summary should reflect the structure of a text. If an article is written in problem-solution order, the summary should include the problem and the solution. But students who use the copy-and-delete method of summarizing often fail to notice the underlying structure of a text, which leaves their summaries—and their comprehension—lacking.

Listing Structure

The listing structure is the least organized text structure and does not always include cue words. In this structure, an idea or object is presented and followed by a list of related ideas or characteristics.

The book *Bridges Are to Cross* by Philemon Sturges (1998) is an example of a picture book organized in listing order. On each page, the author shows a different kind of bridge and, in a few sentences, explains a characteristic or use of the bridge. Each bridge is of equal importance to the next—there are no categories or subcategories within the text.

This structure works well with short, simple texts with few ideas. Talk with students about when it would become difficult for readers. Could you write a bridge-building textbook organized as a list? Why or why not?

The list structure can be a challenge to summarize. When faced with a text in this order, it is easy to get lost in all the details. Knowing how to collapse a list can make summarizing this kind of text easier.

Main Idea Structure

Although not originally described as a text structure, I use this term with students. (Other resources place it as a subcategory of description or listing, which can be confusing.) Many books are organized with main idea structure, and it is the basis for examples in the previous chapter. In this kind of text, a main idea is presented and followed by examples, reasons, or facts. Cue words include *for example, also, in addition,* and so forth.

Your students' social studies or science textbooks are probably organized according to main idea order. Some books will even include a chapter outline or hierarchical map to show how the different ideas relate to one another.

A graphic organizer called a tree map (see Figure 6–3) helps students to see the hierarchy of ideas in a chapter or selection. This kind of organizer allows students to see the relationship of ideas in a visual form. Outlines can be useful as well.

When summarizing text written in main idea order, the strategies from the previous chapter help students to find the main ideas and important details.

Description Structure

Descriptive texts are written to describe an object, event, or idea. One form of description is spatial order, in which a location is described from top to bottom, front to back, and so forth. Readers also encounter descriptive texts organized by sensory details or order of importance.

Because descriptive writing is filled with details, students can have trouble finding the main ideas. Authors of descriptive text often leave the main idea implicit rather than stating it explicitly. Can you infer a main idea from the following paragraph?

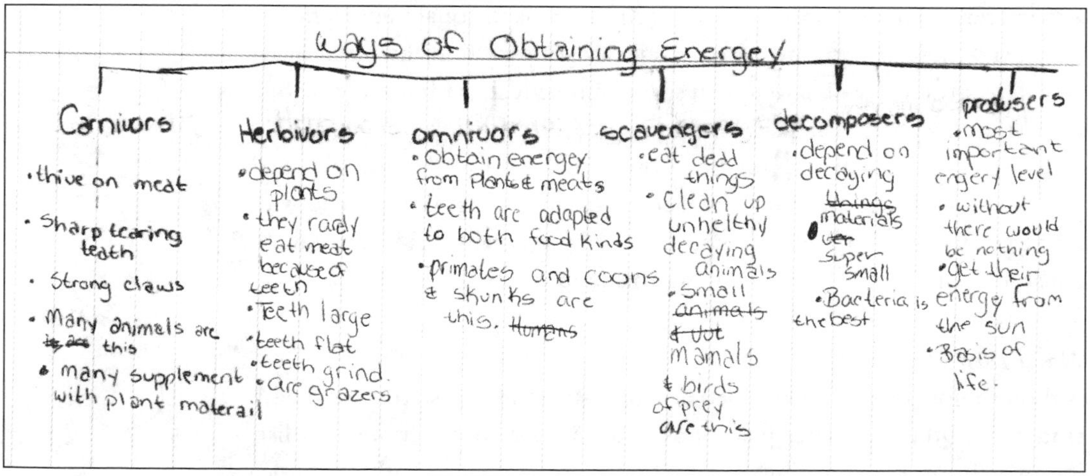

FIGURE 6–3. Tree Map

As my family walked into the water park, I was amazed by all of the fun things we could do. A tall waterslide stood *in the distance*, its cool blue plastic beckoning me for a slippery ride. *To the right*, I saw people drifting along on a lazy river. *Directly in front* of me was a wave pool filled with clear water and fun waves. And a concession stand waited *on my left*, ready to quench my thirst with tall cups of soda. "Let's get started!" I told my mom.

The main idea of this paragraph could be stated, "The water park is amazing." Did you notice the italicized cue words? They help the reader to visualize the relationships among the details.

You can get double instruction from descriptive text by pairing it with the reading strategy of visualizing. Visualizing, or creating sensory images, is an important reading strategy. A reader who visualizes can put herself into the text by imagining the sights, sounds, and feelings. Descriptive text is well suited to teaching this reading strategy. The picture book *Sierra* by Diane Siebert (1996), a lovely example of descriptive writing, can be used to teach about descriptive text and visualizing. *Sierra* is a poem describing a mountain and the life upon it. Try reading the book to students without showing the pictures, and ask them to draw what they imagine. Then, ask students to think about the main idea of the book. What is Siebert saying about the mountain? Students can write a one- or two-sentence summary of the book at the bottom of their drawings.

Cause-and-Effect Structure

Cause-and-effect text is just what it sounds like—a text that discusses causes and effects. Sometimes texts will show how one cause has multiple effects, or how several causes contributed to one effect. This kind of text often shows up in history texts and is signaled by cue words such as *consequently, therefore, as a result,* and *because.*

A summary of text written in cause-and-effect order must include both the causes and effects. Here is where students often have problems. Teaching students how to look for the cue words can help them to identify the underlying structure and include correct information in their summaries.

The cause-and-effect structure is also useful in the everyday life of the classroom. When the unexpected happens, take advantage of the teachable moment to help students recognize causes and effects in real life. One day while a student was at a band lesson during science class, some students accidentally spilled vinegar on his desk. As we talked about the situation at the end of class, we wrote a letter to tell the student what had happened:

> You might wonder why your desk smells like vinegar. There are several causes. While Jon was pouring vinegar into the baking soda cup, Tayler, who was across the room, tripped and fell. Jon looked at her, and didn't pay attention to what he was pouring. Then the baking soda and vinegar bubbled out and over and made a big mess on your desk. We tried to clean it up, but Mrs. Kissner is out of the orange spray cleaner. So now your desk smells bad. You can sit in another seat for the rest of the day.

The student enjoyed getting the letter when he returned from band, and the class experienced writing cause-and-effect text.

Problem-and-Solution Structure

In this kind of text, the author lays out a problem, and then shows the steps toward its solution. Problem-and-solution text can relate to real facts and events that have already occurred, or can be hypothetical discussions of how a problem can be solved. For this reason, problem-and-solution text often shows up on the editorial page of newspapers.

Students sometimes have problems finding the difference between cause-and-effect and problem-and-solution text. This is because both can use the same clue words. The critical thinking required to determine whether a text is cause and effect or problem and solution is a wonderful way to help students consider the macrolevel meaning of a text. Encourage these conversations!

A River Ran Wild by Lynne Cherry (1992) is a classic example of problem-and-solution text. Cherry takes readers through the history of human life along the Nashua River in New Hampshire, from its original beauty to eventual decline. Then she explains how citizens banded together to revive the river.

Comparison Structure

Comparison text examines similarities and differences between objects, people, or events. (This structure is also called *compare and contrast.* However, to compare means to consider the differences as well as the similarities.) Most students have experience reading and writing this kind of text structure. Cue words include *similar, different, the same as, on the other hand, however,* and *yet.* Comparison text can be written in an *alter-*

nating format, with the author switching back and forth between characteristics of the two objects, or in *clustered* format, with the author listing the details of one object, and then all the details about the other.

Many struggling readers will mistake comparison text for description, especially when it is written in the clustered style. They will see the details that describe a topic, but will miss the underlying thread of the author's point. Students sometimes also miss the fact that the similarities and details add up to a general statement. Authors aren't just making a list of what two things have in common, but are using the details to demonstrate a main point.

Graphic organizers for comparing and contrasting are almost too common. Students are used to filling in the lines dutifully on a Venn diagram or double-bubble chart without thinking about the main ideas. The exercise can become just a detail hunt.

Help students to think about the main ideas of compare-and-contrast text by engaging them in the writing process. Intermediate learners benefit from concrete experiences just as much as younger students, and I borrowed a time-tested multisensory lesson from my mother, Karen Pearce. First I gave each student a Hershey Hug and a Hershey Kiss, along with the instructions not to eat them yet! Then students worked in groups to compare and contrast the two candies. They examined the wrappers, smelled the chocolate, and cut the pieces in half. Students can find some amazing tiny details!

While they worked, they recorded their details using whichever graphic organizer they liked. Finally, we compiled their observations. I used a computer hooked up to a projector for an interactive writing session. Students volunteered to contribute sentences, add ideas, or make changes. Together, we worked together to write one paragraph in clustered style, and one paragraph in alternating style. At first, students wanted to use the topic sentence *Hershey Kisses and Hershey Hugs are similar, yet different.* This is a common first attempt. With some prompting, one student added, "Even though they look different, I want to eat them both!" This was a main idea we could use.

Clustered Paragraph.   Notice that all the information about Hershey Kisses is at the beginning, and all of the information about Hershey Hugs is at the end. Transitions like *on the other hand* connect the ideas. As we wrote this paragraph, I guided students toward parallel construction. Notice that the details about each candy are listed in the same order—first the candy's composition, then the candy's wrapping, and finally the way that the candy is made.

Hershey Kisses and Hershey Hugs are similar, yet different. Hershey Kisses are pure milk chocolate. They are wrapped in solid silver foil and are made by dropping liquid chocolate onto a sheet. Hershey Hugs, on the other hand, are made of milk chocolate and white chocolate. Instead of being wrapped in silver foil, they are wrapped in brown and silver-striped foil. Finally, Hershey Hugs are made by putting chocolate in a mold. Whatever their differences, both candies are delicious!

Alternated Paragraph.   This paragraph moves point by point through the comparison. Because the ideas shift back and forth so often, more transitions are needed. As with the clustered paragraph, parallel construction is used.

Two little candies sit in front of me, begging me to eat them. The Hershey Kiss is wrapped in plain silver foil, whereas the Hershey Hug is wrapped in foil of silver and brown. Both are decorated by a cute white tag. When I unwrap the candies, I see that the Hershey Kiss is solid milk chocolate. On the other hand, the Hershey Hug is striped with white chocolate. Both candies have the same shape, but the flat bottom of the Hershey Hug tells me that it was made in a mold, whereas the Hershey Kiss was dropped on a sheet. My taste buds tell me that both candies are delicious!

When you find examples of comparison text for students to use, be sure to start with high-quality texts. Look for comparisons written with parallel construction, transitions to connect details, and a clear main idea.

Chronological Order.   Chronological order can also be called *time order.* Events progress from beginning to end, start to finish. Cue words such as *next, first, finally, second, later,* and *eventually* help a reader to recognize chronological order.

Students find chronological order fairly easy to identify. After all, it's the way we live our lives. Because stories are written in chronological order, students experience this text structure whenever they open up a novel or read a short story.

Expository text written in chronological order can be problematic for students, however. Students used to the narrative structure of a character experiencing a conflict may not recognize that the steps in cell division are also organized in chronological order. And every teacher knows that a series of directions written in chronological order can be quite challenging for students to follow, especially when the directions are interspersed with other bits of information.

Although text written in chronological order is all around us, it is not always of the highest quality. When you look for text to use with students, be sure to start with texts that use many transitions, progress clearly from start to finish, and add limited amounts of extra information. The following is a short paragraph about studying a stream. Can you find the transitions that show the change in time?

Stream Study Steps

You can easily make a stream study kit. Start off with a gallon-size zipper bag. At a discount store, get an aquarium net, some plastic cups, a pack of paintbrushes, and an ice cube tray. (Yes, paintbrushes!) A hand lens is also useful, and a notebook to record your observations.

After you have made your kit, you are ready to find a stream. Be sure to get adult permission and check for safety hazards before you venture into the water! Once you are sure that everything is safe, find a comfortable spot close to the water to settle your belongings.

Begin by filling up the ice cube tray with water. The different compartments in the tray will provide lots of places to keep your little stream creatures separated. Otherwise, they may eat one another!

Next, take the paintbrush and aquatic net. Find a part of the stream with rocks and a slower flow. Carefully turn over a rock. What do you see?

If you're lucky, you'll see a crayfish darting away from you, swimming backward. But you might not see any creatures at first. This doesn't mean that they aren't there. Carefully observe the underside of the rock. Do you see any movement? Make your paintbrush wet and gently try to remove any of the tiny creatures you see. Dip the paintbrush into a compartment of the ice cube tray and watch your find swim away. After you have observed the creature carefully, check the pictures on the survey page to identify what you have caught.

Text structure is an important part of reading instruction. How can we help students to look for structures in texts, and use that knowledge of structure to create a summary?

Teaching Text Structure

Text Structure Poster.   We often assume that students make connections that just aren't happening. I try to foster these connections by giving students record sheets to keep track of texts we read and their underlying structures (Figure 6–4). By comparing texts that they read throughout the year, students become more adept at identifying text structures.

Text Rewrites.   Teaching students that information can be organized in a variety of ways can also help students to internalize text structures. For example, in a unit on biography, I asked students to use the information from the original text (written in chronological order) and reorganize it into a paragraph with another structure. A student who had read about Jackie Robinson wrote a paragraph in cause-and-effect order about the effects of Robinson entering the Major League, whereas a student who read about Abraham Lincoln used spatial order to describe his boyhood home. This helps to emphasize that pieces of writing with the same topic can have different main ideas.

Students can also rewrite texts using additional text features. This works well with chronological order text. Students can take a passage written in chronological order—for example, the previous stream study passage—and rewrite it as a numbered list. Discuss how the numbered list makes the passage look and read differently. Are the events easier to follow? Is the text more effective? Which chronological order texts would not work well for this?

Text Structure Picture Book Activity.   This activity involves all students in reading a picture book and determining text structure. In your school library or book room, gather a variety of picture books. (A list of possibilities is included at the end of the chapter.) You may be lucky enough to have multiple copies of titles, but single copies could work also. Be sure that the picture books reflect a variety of text structures.

I use the book *Everglades* by Jean Craighead George (1997) to model this activity before students begin. I put an overhead transparency of Text Structure Picture Book Activity (Figure 6–5) in front of the students and begin. We start by recording the title of the book—don't forget to underline!—and the copyright information. I have learned that the more I ask students to record copyright information as a routine, the easier it is for them to find this information to create bibliographies and works-cited lists. I ask a student to come to the front and preview the

Text Structures		
Text structure	**Cue words**	**Examples from our reading**
Listing	None	
Description	Location words: in front of, behind, near, etc.	
Main idea	for example, another reason, also, the most important . . . , etc. often uses subheadings or outlines	
Cause and effect	because of, a cause for, an effect of, as a result, consequently	
Problem and solution	a problem is, a solution is, because of, as a result, consequently, therefore	
Chronological order	first, next, eventually, later, finally, then, after, before	

FIGURE 6–4.

Text Structure Picture Book Activity

_____ Record information about your article

Title of book _____

Copyright date _____

Author _____

_____ Preview the book. Make a list of text features that you notice.

_____   _____   _____

_____   _____   _____

_____ Predict the main text structure of the book. Write a sentence to explain your prediction.

____Listing   ____Description   ____Main idea

____Cause/effect   ____Problem/solution   ____Chronological order

_____

_____

_____ With your group, read the book. Listen for any of the text structure cue words. Record them below.

_____

_____

_____ Look back to your prediction about text structure.
Was it accurate? Why or why not?
Discuss your thinking with your group.

_____ After you have finished reading, work with your group to determine the overall structure of the text. (Remember that a text can have individual paragraphs that don't fit the overall structure.) On another piece of paper, write a paragraph to explain your choice. Be sure to include words like main idea, cue words, and text structure in your response.

_____ Work with your group to write a summary of the book. Remember that your summary should reflect the structure of the text. (But don't say, "The structure of the text was . . ."!)

FIGURE 6–5.

text for us. Then I model using the text features to generate a prediction about the text structure of the book. For example, while I was reading *Everglades*, I said, "I notice that each page tells about plants and animals of the Everglades. I predict that this book is written as description, and that I will learn how the plants and animals of the Everglades are unique and special." As I read the book aloud, students record the cue words for the text structure. After we finish reading the book, we reflect on our initial predictions about the text structure and decide what text structure the book shows. I chose *Everglades* as my model because it includes more than one text structure. The book begins with a combination of chronological order and description, and then moves into cause and effect. Exposing children to a complex example during the modeling stage will help them to deal with these kinds of texts in the group activity. Finally, we work as a group to write a summary of the book.

After I model the activity, I arrange students into groups and give each of them their own copy of the activity sheet. This is a good opportunity to use mixed-ability groups. I hold up the books I have selected from the book room and talk briefly about each one, and then allow the groups to choose their books. Building some opportunity for choice into every activity helps to keep intermediate learners engaged and empowered.

Asking a group of five students to share a single copy of a text can lead to some problems. If you are working with single copies, be sure to talk about how to share the reading to ensure that all students pay attention to the book. While students work through the activity, I circulate to listen to their conversations and help as needed.

You may not feel comfortable with grading student summaries just yet. Just because the activity directs them to write a summary doesn't mean that you have to grade it! I often read these summaries, give a few completion points, and jot down notes on how students are doing. Giving students the opportunity to talk with a group about the relationship between text structure and a summary is an important process. It's okay if their products are still not where you want them to be.

Chapter Summary

You can teach students of all reading levels to examine how a text is organized. Teaching about text organization can fit seamlessly into your existing instruction, as you look at the external and internal structures of the stories and articles you already read.

- External structure refers to text features such as subheadings, photographs, and captions. Teach students how to use text features to understand a text and help determine what is important.

- The internal organization, or text structure, is the structure the author uses to organize a text. Common text structures include main idea, compare and contrast, description, listing, problem and solution, and cause and effect.

- Picture books, writing activities, and short reading selections can help students to understand text structure.

Suggested Reading

More Information on Teaching Text Structure

Rhoder, C. 2002. "Mindful Reading: Strategy Instruction That Facilitates Transfer." *Journal of Adolescent & Adult Literacy* 45: 198–213.

Picture Books

Problem and Solution

Cherry, L. 1992. *A River Ran Wild*. San Diego: Gulliver Green Book.

George, J. C. 1997. *Everglades*. New York: HarperCollins.

Chronological

Hayes, J. 1993. *Soft Child: How Rattlesnake Got Its Fangs*. Tucson: Harbinger.

Hollenbeck, K. 1999. *Dancing on the Sand: A Story of an Atlantic Blue Crab*. Norwalk, CT: Soundprints.

Description

Bliss, C. D. 1992. *Matthew's Meadow*. New York: Harcourt.

Siebert, D. 1996. *Sierra*. New York: HarperTrophy.

Listing **67**
Text
Organization

Sturges, P. 1998. *Bridges Are to Cross*. New York: Putnam.

Cause and Effect
Yolen, J. 1995. *Letting Swift River Go*. Boston: Little Brown.

Compare and Contrast
Schuett, S. 1997. *Somewhere in the World Right Now*. New York: Knopf.

7

PARAPHRASING AND COLLAPSING LISTS

"Mrs. Kissner, is this right?" a student asked. I moved to where Megan sat at the round media center table. We were in the library, taking notes for animal reports. Whenever I take a class to the library for research, it seems as if I am pulled in all directions, answering questions of all sorts from all over the room.

"Let me see," I said, trying to focus on Megan while still keeping an eye on the students working at the computers. "You're researching the peregrine falcon?"

"Yes," she said, and showed me her page of notes. Every line was filled with her round, loopy purple handwriting.

I frowned. "Megan, this seems to be exactly what was in the encyclopedia. You were supposed to put the ideas into your own words."

"Well, yes. I thought I'd copy everything and change it later."

Sound familiar? Every time I worked with research reports, I ran into these kinds of difficulties. Some students would simply copy everything onto their papers. Others would print out page after page from the Internet, and still others would produce no notes at all. My students suffered from a lack of paraphrasing skills.

This problem didn't just show up when we wrote reports, either. Not being able to paraphrase also hindered their ability to write summaries and answer open-ended literature questions. Students either copied large portions of the text or eliminated key ideas altogether.

Because short-answer responses to literature questions are an important component of our state testing, our faculty spent many hours trying to come up with ways to improve student responses. Although these efforts were well intentioned, many of them missed the point. Using different-colored highlighters to mark text evidence, ending each lesson with a stance question, putting the correct "cue words" at the end of our reading questions—none of these actions led to much improvement. What my students needed to learn was how to paraphrase.

Not only is paraphrasing an important skill in its own right, but it is also a necessary component of summarizing. If students are to write the main ideas of a piece of text, they must be able to restate those main ideas in their own words.

Paraphrasing sounds easy, but as anyone else who has labored in a school library with students taking research notes can tell you, paraphrasing can require significant brain power. College professor David Maas (2002) quipped, "Paraphrasing takes a great deal of cerebral energy. If a student does it correctly, his forehead should feel hot enough to fry an egg" (198). In fact, poor paraphrasing skills are partially the root of plagiarism. When students of any age are confronted by an idea that they can't put into their own words, the temptation to copy sometimes proves overwhelming.

Is paraphrasing simply regurgitation? Some teachers and researchers think so. But as I've worked through teaching paraphrasing in the classroom, I've learned that it is a much deeper process. In a way, paraphrasing *is* understanding. If you can restate an idea or concept in your own words, you have made it your own; it has become something that you understand. After reading a difficult passage, I'll often try to restate the ideas in my own words as a way to test my understanding.

To help Megan and the rest of my students, I decided to consider my own strategies for paraphrasing. How did I learn this skill? I recalled a third grade teacher who made us read a passage, close the encyclopedia, and then write down what we remembered. Although this eliminated the urge to copy, it also bred frustration. I remember focusing so much on trying to remember how to spell Guglielmo Marconi's first name that I forgot the idea I was trying to write down in the first place. Besides that one experience, I couldn't think of any teacher who explicitly taught paraphrasing. I learned through trial and error.

To figure out what strategies I found useful, I started with a text about the great auk. As I read the text and wrote my own version, I found myself doing three main things: changing the words, changing the order, and changing the structure of the author's words.

I focused on one paragraph of simple text:

> Sailors had a host of uses for the clumsy birds. They herded them on deck to provision long voyages, collected their feathers for hats, and even used the fatty bodies as fuel. The last known pair of great auks was killed in 1844, but scientists didn't realize that the entire species was extinct for many years.

The first sentence can be paraphrased by changing the words. I thought about "a host of" and what I could substitute for that phrase:

Sailors had *many* uses for the great auk.

To paraphrase the second sentence, I changed the words and the order of the list:

The fatty bodies were used as fuel, the feathers used for hats, and the birds themselves were brought on board to feed the sailors on lengthy trips.

Finally, I altered the structure of the third sentence. In its original form, it is a compound sentence; here, it is rewritten as a complex sentence:

It took scientists many years to realize that the last known pair of great auks had been killed in 1844.

These three strategies—changing the words, order, and structure—are often used by readers as they paraphrase. Skillful readers subconsciously blend all three, seamlessly using the strategies to restate text in their own words.

Notice that paraphrasing does not necessarily condense the text. Students seemed to learn best when I taught them how to paraphrase first, and then taught how to condense our paraphrased sentences into notes. In its general form, though, a paraphrase of a text can be just as long as the original and still be perfectly acceptable. (These guidelines are suggested for general classroom use as students discuss and make meaning of text. If you are working with upper level students to generate reports, be sure to explain when they need to cite the original author of the ideas.)

After focusing on paraphrasing for several days, I bravely ventured back into the library with my students to work on the animal reports. "How is it going, Megan?" I asked. I was almost afraid to look at her paper.

"Is this right?" she said. This time, I saw the same purple loopy handwriting. Instead of text copied out of the encyclopedia, however, I saw her own words, complete with smiley-faced bullets to separate the ideas.

"Great job, Megan," I praised her.

Ideas for Teaching Paraphrasing

You can teach paraphrasing with every text, every day. Here are some places to start.

When I began working with students, I taught them the three main strategies that we used. Keeping the strategies posted on the board, we slowly went through the process. I worried at first that this would be ineffective. As you can see from the following excerpt, it requires us to consider a text word by word, sentence by sentence. I feared that I was becoming a painfully boring teacher! However, when I saw the improvement in my students' work, I realized the effort was worthwhile.

Together, we read "The Karner Blue Butterfly" (Figure 7–1). Before we began paraphrasing, I put the heading Key Words on the board and asked students to name key words from the article. These words can't be replaced by synonyms. For example, we have to refer to the Karner blue butterfly by its specific name. Calling it "the sapphire insect" would not express the same meaning.

Even students of lower ability can find key words in a text. Our list included Karner blue butterfly, pine barrens, habitat, and environment.

Next, I put some important sentences from the article on the overhead projector. One sentence was "The pine barrens that remain exist in small, isolated fragments."

ME: Can we take out the words *pine barrens*?

STUDENT 1: No, it's a key word in the text.

ME: So we'll need to leave that. I'll write 'The pine barrens.' What about *that remain*? Can I replace this with words that have a similar meaning?

STUDENT 2: That have stayed?

STUDENT 3: That are left?

ME: Let's go with 'that are left.' So now I have 'The pine barrens that are left.' What can I do about the rest of the sentence?

STUDENT 2: Maybe you could put, 'are small.'

STUDENT 1: But it's not that they're small, they're not around anything else. They're all isolated. They're all by themselves.

ME: Not connected?

STUDENT 2: Let's put that. 'The pine barrens that are left are small and not connected.'

The Karner Blue Butterfly

Adapted from USFWS "The Karner Blue Butterfly"

http://northeast.fws.gov/factshee.html

Walk into one of nature's unique ecosystems in the northeast, a pine barren, on a still, hot July day. You'll smell the aroma of pine. You'll sense the dryness of the air. If you are lucky, you'll see the fluttering of small iridescent blue wings. You're in one of the very few places where you can see the rare Karner blue butterfly—in one of the northeastern pine barrens of New York and New Hampshire.

What is it?

The Karner blue butterfly (*Lycaedes melissa samuelis*) is a small butterfly. Its wingspan is only about one inch. The male's wings are marked with a silvery or dark blue color.

Karner blues are found in the northern range of wild lupine habitat. Wild lupine (*Lupinus perennis*) is a small flowering plant found in pine barrens and oak savannas. These habitats occur in New Hampshire, New York, Michigan, Wisconsin, Indiana, and Minnesota.

The Karner blue likes to live in areas of pitch pines and scrub oaks mixed with grassy fields. The wildfires that burned through the pine barrens helped to keep the habitat suitable for the Karner blue. There used to be many of these kinds of places in a narrow band across ten states. Today, the Karner blue can no longer be found in five of these states.

Why are they so rare?

As people have stopped wildfires and built communities, the habitat of the Karner blue has been lost. The pine barrens that remain exist in small, isolated fragments. This keeps the Karner blue from moving and spreading.

New York's Albany Pine Bush once covered as much as 40,000 acres. Today, only 2,000 acres remain. All around, people have built houses and towns, opened sand and gravel mines, and turned pine barrens into pine plantations. The Karner blue has specific needs and cannot adapt to living so close to humans.

Why should we be concerned?

Since the Pilgrims landed in 1620, more than 500 species and varieties of our nation's plants and animals have become extinct. This loss of biodiversity is continuing. Each and every species has a valuable role in the balance of nature. Each loss disturbs that fragile balance. Once a species is extinct, it is lost forever.

We have learned that many plants and animals are useful to humans as sources of food and medicine. With the loss of each species, we lose a potential resource for improving the quality of life for all people.

Also, some species of plants and animals may show us whether their environment is healthy. The Karner blue butterfly's disappearance from fragile pine barren habitat tells us that something is wrong. Protecting pine barrens will affect not only the Karner blue butterfly, but also many other special plants and animals.

What you can do to help

Learn more about the Karner blue butterfly and other rare and endangered plants and animals. The US Fish and Wildlife Service, state wildlife agencies, and private conservation organizations are working on programs for protection and management of the Karner blue butterfly.

FIGURE 7–1.

Once we have done a few sentences as a whole class, students work in small groups and on their own to paraphrase sentences. Paraphrasing requires teacher brainpower as well! Often, I need to think quickly about whether to accept and praise an approximation, or correct misguided thinking. One example is with the passage,

> The Karner blue butterfly (*Lycaedes melissa samuelis*) is a small butterfly. Its wingspan is only about one inch. The male's wings are marked with a silvery or dark blue color.

One group's paraphrase read, "The small butterfly Karner blue is one inch long." I had a quick decision to make—simply accept their sentence as a good step forward or point out the slight difference between length and wingspan. Was it just splitting hairs or was it a legitimate problem? I decided that the difference between length and wingspan was worth discussing. Students were about to begin writing reports of endangered animals and would probably encounter different measurements in their research. Once I sketched a rough butterfly and showed students the length and the wingspan, they discovered the problem with their sentence on their own and made the necessary correction. Depending on your situation, students, and text, you may choose to tolerate some par aphrased sentences that show progress but are not exactly accurate. As long as you keep the end in mind, the students will improve.

This kind of direct instruction doesn't have to take an entire class period. I've used paraphrasing as an effective transition activity by putting a sentence or two on the board for students to paraphrase at the start of class. In math class, I sometimes ask students to read a set of directions, and then paraphrase the directions into their learning logs. When we discuss students' work, I emphasize the strategies of changing the words, changing the structure, and changing the order.

Other ways to improve student paraphrasing involve zeroing in on one of the three strategies mentioned earlier.

Vocabulary Instruction

In order for students to change the words in an idea, they need to have a ready arsenal of synonyms at their command. Students don't always have the words to express their thinking. In the previous example, the students' vocabularies weren't sophisticated enough to distinguish the difference between length and wingspan.

There are many quick and easy vocabulary activities that can be integrated into other lessons. The key words portion of the previous lesson can help a teacher find student vocabulary gaps. If a student lists a common word as a key word in the article, that word probably needs more explanation.

A linear array is one way to show students the shades of difference among related words. In our study of endangered and extinct animals, for example, we looked at the words *rare, endangered, common, abundant, extinct,* and *uncommon.* I wrote these words on notecards and handed the cards to several students. I told the students to arrange themselves in order from a word that describes an animal they are likely to see, to a word that describes an animal they are unlikely to see. This activity led to a conversation about the difference between *rare* and *endangered*, and how we had to be careful when substituting one word for another.

Linear arrays are also useful when teaching fiction. Many open-ended reading questions ask students to identify a character's traits or emotions. Showing students the many alternatives to *angry—furious, irritated, mad, miffed, livid,* and so forth—helps them to be more precise when answering these questions, and helps them to find other words to paraphrase quickly what the author says in the text.

Semantic mapping is another way to help students become aware of the connections between words. I teach students how to create my version of a semantic map at the beginning of the year, and then use it as a homework assignment for spelling and reading. Besides helping students become familiar with words, the semantic map also improves their dictionary and thesaurus use. The semantic map that I use in my classroom includes the target word at the center, definition, synonyms, related words, and the target word used in a sentence. (I explain the related words as words with the same root, such as *value* and *valuable*.) Other teachers add antonyms and word associations to the list as well. While reading about Mount Everest, Liz chose her own vocabulary words for making semantic maps (Figure 7–2).

A fun way to improve student vocabulary is to offer a vocabulary word of the day or week. This becomes an easy routine and time filler for students who finish assignments early. I post directions for Vocabulary Word of the Week on the chalkboard, along with an interesting new word for the students. The rules are simple. On a slip of paper, the student copies the word, paraphrases the definition, and writes a sentence using the word.

In the middle of the school year, I often allow students to take over the task of running Vocabulary Word of the Week. They choose the word

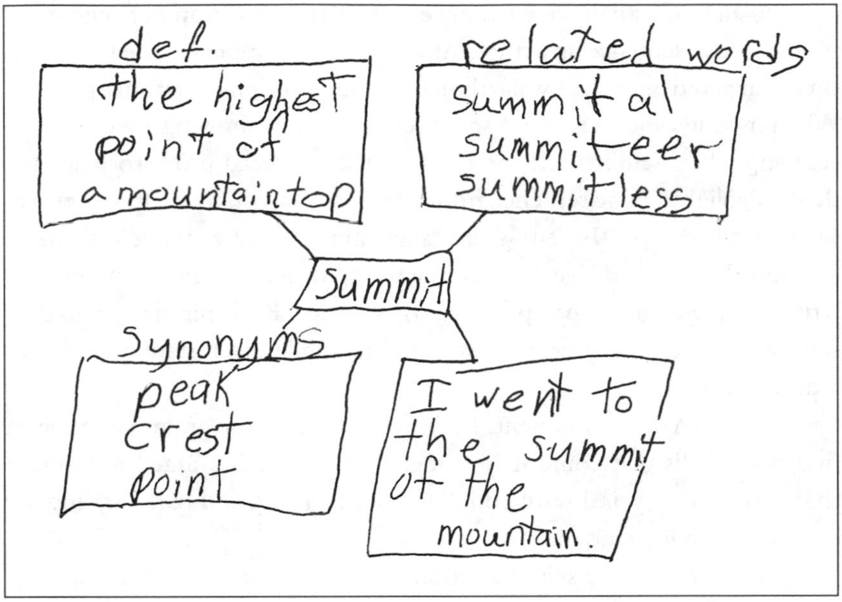

FIGURE 7–2. Liz's Semantic Map

for the week, read the submissions, and decide if each submission is correct. Putting students in charge allows for some powerful conversations. I knew that I was making progress when I was called to mediate in a dispute between the student managers and another student.

"I have everything on my entry, but Andrew says I can't win," Jacob complained.

Thomas had the dictionary open in front of him. "You have to put the definition in your own words. You just copied it. Look."

Jacob read the dictionary definition and looked back to his paper. "It's not exactly the same. I changed a word."

"That's just the same as copying," Thomas said. "Isn't it, Mrs. Kissner?"

I didn't know what to say. I was so happy—two sixth graders, arguing about paraphrasing, going back to the dictionary, looking at the directions. In the classroom, it doesn't get much better than this.

Grammar Applications

Students don't just have trouble with changing the words in a text, however. Sometimes they cannot see how to change the structure or order. This is where grammar skills can help.

A student actually opened my eyes to the connection between paraphrasing and sentence structure. After students completed their research on endangered animals, I walked them through the entire writing process. When it came time to revise, I spent several lessons showing them how to rearrange their sentences. I modeled on the overhead projector and students highlighted one sentence from a body paragraph to try to rearrange. Derrick called out, "Isn't this the same thing we were doing with paraphrasing?" I realized that he was exactly right. Rearranging sentences as writers is the same as paraphrasing as a reader. Both require an understanding of the idea to be expressed and the ability to restate that idea in a different way.

After Derrick's comment, I skimmed through the grammar guide to find other skills that could help students with paraphrasing. I found one that was fairly easy and resulted in improved writing and paraphrasing for even lower ability students.

A quick and easy skill that instantly translates into summary writing is the use of the appositive. Consider this paragraph from the article about the Karner Blue: *Karner blues are found in the northern range of wild lupine habitat. Wild lupine (Lupinus perennis) is a small flowering plant found in pine barrens and oak savannas.* A way to change the structure of this paragraph is to use a structure called an *appositive*. Basically stated, an appositive is a noun or noun phrase that renames another noun: *The Karner blue lives in the habitat of the wild lupine, a small flowering plant.* The explanation of the wild lupine has been combined into the sentence about the butterfly's habitat.

I frequently use the appositive structure when I write. However, I'd never taught it to my students, considering it a higher level grammar skill. But the students picked it up fairly easily. I modeled sentences from the rough drafts of their reports. *The Eastern Massasauga is a kind of rattlesnake. It can be found in Pennsylvania.* Students soon saw how they could rewrite the two sentences as *A kind of rattlesnake, the Eastern Massasauga can be found in Pennsylvania.* Knowing the appositive structure is an effective way to condense sentences in a paraphrased text.

The appositive is useful in paraphrasing fiction as well. Students can use the structure to express information quickly about a character. For example, *"Karrie, an eighth grade student, must choose between her best friend and her cousin."*

Paraphrasing Instruction Produces Results

The effect of teaching paraphrasing was evident in student reports, answers to questions, and even their writing. Students began to realize that there are many ways to express ideas. The time that I had invested in teaching paraphrasing was well worthwhile.

Easy Sentences for Beginning Instruction

My experience showed me that starting with short, easily read sentences helps the students to grasp the concept of paraphrasing most quickly. This is a time to use more EPR. I distribute a small whiteboard and marker to each student, and then put sentences like the following on the chalkboard or overhead projector. Students then work to paraphrase the sentences.

- Students will find that it is enjoyable to study different genres of literature.

- Mysteries, thrillers, and suspense novels are read by many people each year.

- The word *genre* refers to a type of literature. Understanding what different genres are like can help you to comprehend what you read.

Is This an Accurate Paraphrase?

Students enjoy playing this as a kind of game. On the overhead projector, I show them the original text and the paraphrase, and they have to choose whether the paraphrase is accurate. To make things livelier, I direct them to perform a different action for each set—thumbs up, thumbs down, stand up, sit down, go to the left or right side of the room, and so forth.

- *Original text:* Realistic fiction books describe characters that are like people you may know. In realistic fiction, the conflict and events could really happen.

  Paraphrase: Realistic fiction books have real people and events that really happened. (not accurate)

- *Original text:* In historical fiction books, the setting is very important. These books take place in the past and may include both real and made-up characters. Authors of historical fiction research real events and time periods to include authentic details in their stories.

Paraphrase: Historical fiction books take place in the past and may include real characters and events as well as made-up ones. (accurate, although not very good)

- *Original text:* A biography is a story of a real person's life, written by another person. An autobiography is a story of a real person's life, written by that person.

  Paraphrase: Biographies and autobiographies both tell about someone's life. Different people write them. (not accurate)

- *Original text:* Nonfiction text is text that is written to inform. It includes only true facts and details, and describes a real subject.

  Paraphrase: Text that includes only true facts and details, and is written to inform is called nonfiction text. (accurate)

Paraphrasing is a crucial skill for writing summaries. If students cannot put text into their own words, they do not understand what they read. Teaching all students how to paraphrase will help them in reading class and beyond.

Collapsing Lists

I've given summary ratings and checklists to other teachers in my school. Most of them come back with the same question. "I like the parts about main idea and deleting trivia . . . but what does it mean to collapse a list?"

Not many people have heard of collapsing lists. But this is an important skill for summary writing. It's also fun to teach!

Collapsing a list is similar to both paraphrasing and inferring a main idea. As with paraphrasing, the reader must take ideas from the text and change the wording. As with inferring a main idea, the reader must analyze a list of details and create a general statement.

Why, then, is collapsing a list considered a separate skill? The difference is that a main idea is stated as a sentence, whereas a collapsed list may be just a word or phrase. Also, lists can function as details in a piece of text.

When students cannot collapse lists, they either list all the items or omit the idea altogether. Students who are ready to work on this skill will sometimes collapse a list inefficiently, using a word that doesn't quite describe all the members of the group. A quick way to assess your students' abilities is to put some lists on the overhead projector and see what they can come up with. I was surprised when I put *whipped cream, cherries, chocolate syrup,* and *peanuts* on the overhead projector. "Candy?" one student asked. "Dessert!" called another. I had thought that *ice cream toppings* was fairly obvious. I knew that we needed more work with this idea.

Beginning Activities to Collapse Lists

These lists are good to help build students' confidence. I borrowed heavily from our reading selections and concepts that students were studying in science, social studies, and math. Sometimes I put several lists on the overhead projector for students to think about at the beginning of class; sometimes we turned it into a game like *$25,000 Pyramid*.

- Sapphires, rubies, diamonds, emeralds: gems

- Multiplication, division, addition, subtraction: operations

- Rain, snow, sleet, hail: precipitation

- Stamp collecting, scrapbooking, making models: hobbies

- Paleontologist, biologist, chemist, physicist: scientists

- Sleeping bag, tent, lantern: camping supplies

- Pencil, pen, marker: writing utensils

More Difficult Lists

Students are often faced with lists of items that are not so clearly defined. To help students collapse these lists, I started by adding some items to previous lists so that students needed to expand their categories. For example, if I add *paperclips* to the writing utensil list, it can't be called *writing utensils* anymore. It needs a broader title, such as *office supplies*.

Readers do not just need to collapse lists of objects. Collapsing a list of events is important as well. When my students were reading biographies, we used a short selection about the early career of journalist Nellie Bly as a shared reading. Students had to answer the question, "Do you admire Nellie Bly? Why or why not?"

I was disappointed by how many of the students' responses focused on tiny details—Nellie Bly went into the insane asylum, she was fired from a factory for getting a drink of water. Although these details were valid, the students did not put them together to make a general statement.

The events in a biography, I realized, are just another kind of list for readers to collapse. I made a list of several of Nellie's accomplishments and asked students to write a sentence to collapse the list.

Nellie Bly went into an insane asylum to expose how patients were treated.

Nellie Bly worked in factories to write about the poor working conditions.

Nellie Bly exposed crooked landlords and the terrible condition of the tenements.

Collapsing this list was serious brainwork for my students. Eventually, a few students came up with a sentence like this: "Nellie Bly *made a difference* by writing about problems." The students had looked at each event and created a general statement about Nellie's accomplishments.

To practice the skill further, students listed three to five accomplishments or events from the individual biographies that they were reading and then traded papers with other students. The task was to collapse the list and write a general statement about their partner's historical figure. This wasn't easy. Because students generated the lists, sometimes they were difficult to collapse. However, the conversations that followed proved to be worth the effort.

Collapsing Lists in Real Life

Collapsing lists can also be an effective way to manage tasks for a large group of people. This spring, my sixth graders decided they wanted to undertake some work in our school butterfly garden. I knew that sending students outside to work can be chaotic unless everyone has clearly defined tasks. But what would those tasks be?

The week before our work day, we ventured outdoors with clipboards and pencils. Students were to write down everything they thought we needed to do in the garden. When we returned to class, students met in their table groups and shared lists. Each group received three sentence strips on which to record the tasks that they thought were most important.

After each group was finished, one student read their tasks and posted them on the chalkboard. We grouped related tasks together as we worked. One set read: *pull dead plants, trim weeds, get rid of branches.* Another set read *fix sign, put stepping stones back in order,* and *fill birdbath.*

We talked about how we could collapse these lists to create general work groups. The first set became *Clean up old plant material*. The second set gave students some trouble. Andrew ventured, "Deal with the existing things in the garden?" But that seemed to be too broad. After all, weren't the plants *things*? Laura said, "Could we call it *nonplant items*?" This solved our problem!

Our work groups became *Deal with existing nonplant items, Clean up old plant material, Plant new plants, Clean up trash, and Prepare soil*. The next day, students signed up for the work groups and appropriated equipment. When we went outside, every group knew what tasks to accomplish—thanks to our work at collapsing lists.

Chapter Summary

Whether students are taking notes, writing reports, reading biographies, or even just creating a list of tasks to be done, they will need to use the skills of paraphrasing and collapsing lists.

- To paraphrase is to restate ideas in your own words. Three easy strategies for paraphrasing include changing the order, changing the structure, or changing the words.

- Students need to practice paraphrasing and recognizing accurate paraphrases. Every-pupil-response strategies such as having students write paraphrased sentences on dry-erase boards are easy ways to do this.

- Collapsing a list is simply replacing a long list of related objects, ideas, or events with a general category.

- Put lists of items on an overhead and ask students to collapse the lists.

- As students become more skilled, collapse lists of everyday tasks or events in stories and biographies.

Through formal and informal activities, students can learn the skills they need and become expert paraphrasers.

8 SUMMARIZING NARRATIVE TEXT

Up to this point, most of this book has been about the skills and processes needed for expository summaries. I found that students in my class were able to produce passable summaries of narrative text, so I concentrated my efforts on the area of most weakness: the nonfiction summaries. I didn't think much about summarizing narratives until a colleague came to me, summary rating checklist in hand.

"Maybe I'm missing something," she said. "But I tried to use this checklist when I had my students write summaries of *The Circuit*, and it just didn't work. How can you find the main ideas of a story?"

"I made the checklist for nonfiction," I told her. "Stories don't really have the same kinds of main ideas." Scanning the paper, I added, "I think we'd need to make an entirely new checklist." And I don't have time to make it, I added silently to myself, looking at the pile of ungraded papers that sat on my desk. Now was not the time to start researching a new idea. Besides, I harbored the fear that the faculty would begin to view me as some sort of summary freak.

"Oh," she sighed. "Well, could you make a new checklist, then? Since you're so into summarizing."

Ah, well. Summary freak it was.

I didn't really mind turning my attention to creating a checklist for assessing narrative summaries, however, because a large part of my ungraded pile consisted of the very same. What would I need to change to make the checklist functional? To figure this out, I needed to think about the nature of narrative text, the skills and experiences that students bring to the summarizing task, and, finally, what a summary of fiction should include.

The Nature of Narrative Text

What makes a story a story? The general model is that a story consists of a series of related events, called the *plot*, through which *characters* move to solve a central problem or *conflict*. The story takes place in a specific time and place, called the *setting*, and conveys an underlying message or comment on life, the *theme*.

Within this story structure, the plot consists of several different events. A typical story begins with the exposition, in which the characters and setting are introduced. The conflict begins with the rising action, reaches the point of highest tension at the climax, and slows down with the falling action. The resolution ties up any remaining loose ends.

This is not the only way of thinking about a story, though. A story grammar, more commonly used in the lower grades, identifies specific events more clearly. The story begins with the *initiating event*, something that sets the story in motion. The protagonist responds with an *internal response*, the inner reaction to the initiating event, and makes *attempts* to solve the problem. The attempts have an *outcome*, and the story eventually ends with a *resolution*.

Besides these story elements, narrative texts have some other common characteristics. Narrative texts are usually organized in chronological order. Authors often use signal words like *first, next,* and *then* to show the reader how events are connected. Although we often associate narrative text with fiction, nonfiction genres such as biography and autobiography are also narratives. A narrative can be as simple as a story about what happened in the cafeteria yesterday and as complex as a 300-page novel.

What Students Already Know About Summarizing Narrative Text

Just as reading narrative text is more familiar to students than reading expository text, summarizing narrative text is easier too. Children begin retelling stories even before they enter school. Preschoolers are always ready to tell tales about what they've done, books they've heard, stories they've shared. (My husband and I still remember the time our four-year-old talked nonstop through a two-hour car trip!)

As students enter school, they begin to have experience with formal retelling. Many primary reading programs include retelling as both an instructional strategy and an assessment strategy. After listening to or reading a selection, students are asked to retell the story and are scored on how well they can recount the important events, characters, and conflicts. As you will learn in the next chapter, even just these simple retelling exercises can have a significant effect on student learning. And these retelling experiences are an important first step on the road to summarizing.

Are student summaries of fiction better than their summaries of expository text? The research is contradictory. Some studies find that students produce better summaries of narrative text (Hidi and Anderson 1986). Other studies show that students in fourth and fifth grade have as many problems summarizing narratives as summarizing expository text (Taylor 1986). Students certainly have more experience with narrative text than with expository text. Children naturally love listening to stories, and through these experiences they become accustomed to the typical story structure of the goal-based narrative. Readers don't have to deal with new concepts and an unfamiliar text structure, the theory goes, so they may have more opportunity to comprehend what they are reading. This could lead to better, more sophisticated summaries with greater use of strategies such as paraphrasing, organizing, and generalizing.

Students can still fall prey to the same pitfalls that await them in expository summarizing. Just as in nonfiction text, students reading fiction can have trouble distinguishing between details of textual importance (important to the author) and contextual importance (important to the reader). Paraphrasing can also be a problem for students, especially when a text is heavy in dialogue.

And narrative text poses its own problems. Students who can easily read stories that follow a simple plot structure will have trouble summarizing a more complex story. For example, authors will interrupt the flow of a story with a flashback (events that occur before the main setting of the story) or flashforward (events that occur after the main problem). Books like *Walk Two Moons* (Creech 1994) and *Holes* (Sachar 1998) that use many flashbacks can be difficult for intermediate readers to summarize.

Instead of a main idea, a story has a central problem, or conflict. Students often have difficulty finding the conflict of a story. Sometimes this is because a story includes one or more complications, which makes the central conflict hard to find. Sometimes this is because the conflict is internal, or inside the mind of the protagonist. Some conflicts are hard to find because they are very subtle.

Finally, some students have difficulty summarizing a story that is told in first person. When the story is told in this manner, students need to look to dialogue to infer the name of the narrator. In some stories, the narrator's name is told only once or twice, and a reader may miss it.

So how do these story elements affect a summary checklist? After several attempts, I made a Summary Checklist for fiction that worked well for my students (Figure 8–1).

Summary Checklist
Narrative Text

Name _____ **Date** _____

Title of text _____

		Beginning	Developing	Proficient
Basic Summary Criteria	**Important ideas from the text**	Important ideas are missing OR important ideas aren't stated accurately	Some important ideas are presented, but • Some are missing • Used author's exact words • Doesn't use key words from the text • Events are not in order	Important ideas are presented clearly and in the student's own words
	Accurately paraphrases the author's words	Many inaccurate statements OR copied directly from text	Attempt is made to paraphrase, but • Awkward wording • Best words not chosen	The author's words are accurately and precisely paraphrased
	Deletes trivia and repeated information	Many trivial or unimportant statements included	Some trivial or unimportant statements included	No trivial or unimportant statements included
	Does not include irrelevant statements or opinions	Many irrelevant statements, opinions included (reads more like personal response)	Some irrelevant statements, opinions included	No irrelevant statements, opinions included
	Includes key story elements such as character names, setting, and conflict	Story elements missing, lack of specific detail	Some story elements present, one or more missing	Key story elements are included

Comments:

FIGURE 8–1.

Guidelines for an Effective Summary

Include Important Events

A narrative summary is based on events. Most students don't have trouble coming up with some events from a story. The difficulty lies in selecting the *right* events. As with expository text, sometimes students list events with contextual importance rather than textual importance. This means that students focus on events that evoke a personal response rather than events that are important to the story. With no text features like sub-headings or bold print to guide them, some students get lost in the "and then, and then, and then . . . ."

Which events should be included? There is no hard and fast rule. To some extent, the decision depends upon the purpose and length of the finished summary. Summarizing a novel in one paragraph requires more generalization than summarizing the same novel in three pages. But knowing which events are important also requires an understanding of the conflict of the story, and knowing which events contribute to the development and resolution of the conflict. Here is where collapsing lists becomes important, because many events can be collapsed into one more general event.

When I score student summaries for assessment, I often make a list of the important events to look at while I read the summaries. This helps me to keep the events in mind and see how students' ideas match up with mine. I don't look for perfect matches—sometimes a student will show an interesting insight into a text and deem an event important for a reason I had never considered. Similarly, sometimes students collapse events in a way I had not imagined. Events are important in a story, but simply listing events is not enough to have a good summary.

Accurately Paraphrase an Author's Words

I have found that students are less likely to copy text from a narrative than from a nonfiction article. But, students also tend to skip over dialogue and ignore information that is expressed through conversation. Students also may have trouble with accuracy, and will paraphrase the text in a way that goes far beyond the author's meaning.

Paraphrasing problems in fiction often stem from incorrect inferences. An inference is a guess that a reader makes based on the author's clues and the reader's schema. If students are lacking background information, their inferences can stray from the author's meaning. In the story *The Circuit,* the family drives from place to place in a car affectionately called Carcanchita.

Naming a car was an entirely foreign concept to several of my students, and Carcanchita showed up as a sister in their paraphrased version of the text. Paraphrasing is an important skill for fiction as well as nonfiction.

Delete Trivia and Repeated Information

In a narrative, it can be challenging to separate the trivia from the important details. Sometimes an author deliberately buries information at the beginning of a story, only to have it turn out to be essential to the unraveling of the plot. Other authors pepper their stories with interesting, amusing, but essentially pointless little tidbits. A well-written summary of a narrative should include the details that turn out to be important, but should cast aside those that are just meaningless chatter.

Do Not Include Irrelevant Statements and Opinions

Have you ever read a summary that sounds more like a review or a personal response? Students have trouble with this rule when they are not quite sure of what a summary is. They see other students around them filling a page with writing, and they want to do well, so they write down whatever they can think of. Summaries of narratives should not include advice to the author or characters, opinions of the text, or personal connections.

Include Key Story Elements Such as Character Names, Setting, and Conflict

A well-written narrative summary cannot be simply a listing of events. To show a developed understanding of a text, a summary needs some mention of the important story elements. Of course, character names should always be used. The setting does not always have to be mentioned, unless it is integral to the plot—historical fiction, for instance. Conflict, of course, is very important to the summary, because it underlies the events of the plot.

What about theme? For a time, I was certain that a summary of fiction had to include the theme. Now I'm not so sure. Some texts, especially easy ones, just don't have an explicit theme or deeper meaning. Trying to write a sentence to state the theme of these stories only makes the summary sound awkward. But the summary should still include some kind of generalization about how the situation at the end of the story was different from the situation at the beginning of the story, even if this generalization is so simple as to say that a character's feelings changed.

Using the Checklist

Like the nonfiction checklist, the fiction checklist can be used for both initial and ongoing assessment. When I wanted to find out how well my students could summarize easy fiction, I gave them the story "Sandbox Archaeologist" (Figure 8–2). I had written this story as a model for seventh graders during a short story unit in a previous year.

I gave it to my sixth graders without any prereading activities. Although I was pleased to see that most of them could find that the narrator of the first-person story was named Gwen, I was surprised to find that half the class didn't recognize "Gwen" as a girl's name! I wonder if Gwen's archaeological aspirations confirmed their initial inferences that Gwen was a boy, and I jotted down a note to myself to think about a lesson about inferring the gender of a narrator. (Every lesson leads to more ideas!)

This is a fairly simple story. The conflict is Gwen versus herself—in some ways, Gwen versus boredom. She doesn't get to go to camp so she needs to find something else that is interesting to do. There is an implicit theme that good things can come from initial disappointment. Gwen didn't get what she wanted, but she finds that backyard archaeology might be even more fun than camp.

The important events of this story include the following: Gwen's older brother goes to camp, Gwen gets a book about archaeology, Gwen starts digging in the backyard, Gwen finds and displays artifacts, and Gwen's brother returns and is a little jealous of what Gwen has been doing.

The first item on the checklist, "includes important events," can be a good starting point. A student who cannot pick out the key events of a story will need work with story structure and events. This can be seen in Sarah's response (Figure 8–3). Although she attempted to complete the task, she wasn't sure which events should be included in the summary. She will need to work on how to choose which events are most important.

Sarah also focused on the trivial episode of the chicken bone. She seemed to have missed the ending of the story, and could work on looking for the resolution or solution.

What did Sarah do well? She used the name of the important character and kept her summary brief. When I talked with Sarah about her summary, I started by discussing these strong points before we looked at what could be improved.

A good understanding of the events of a story does not necessarily mean that the student fully comprehends what happened. This is evident

Sandbox Archaeologist

In the summer that my brother went to camp, I got a book about archaeology.

I was not impressed.

"Great. William gets to go sleep in a tent and go on hikes, and I get a stupid book," I complained.

"I thought that you would like the book, Gwen," Mom said, and I felt guilty. I knew she couldn't afford to send us both to camp.

Besides, I did like archaeology. I spent the next day reading.

"Did you know that archaeologists have to divide a place where they're working into grids?" I asked my mom the next morning. "A grid is made up of lines and markers—it looks kind of like your waffle," I added.

"Interesting," Mom murmured, sipping her coffee.

"And archaeologists have to use tiny shovels and sometimes even paintbrushes so they don't damage what they find," I continued.

"Fascinating."

"And I think I'm going to dig up the backyard and see if I can find some artifacts."

"Amazing...wait a sec." Mom looked up. "I don't like the sound of this."

"But Mom! You're the one who got me the book!" I protested. "It would be a good project for me."

"Gwen," Mom said firmly, "I'm not having you tear up the backyard."

"Well," I said. "What if I move the sandbox, and dig there? We haven't played in it for two years."

She couldn't find a reason to say no. "I guess," she said. "But you won't find anything."

"Why not?"

"Our house wasn't built until 1965," she explained. "There's nothing very old to find."

But instead of giving up, I went to the library.

"Do you have any old maps of the town?" I asked Mrs. Shultz.

She grinned at me. "Gwen, I wish you'd come in here with easy questions," she said. "Like where's the children's section and what time does the library close? Instead you want old maps. Well, let's see what we have."

After fifteen minutes of searching she pulled out a dusty, yellowed book. It had maps of our entire town from 1877.

"Your house is one block off Main Street, isn't it?" Mrs. Shultz said. We looked at the map. There was no house at my corner.

I swallowed my disappointment. First no camp, now no archaeology.

"But here's something interesting," Mrs. Shultz said. "Look, the blacksmith's shop was right here, on Main Street."

"That's half a block away," I said.

"But back then, when things broke, people couldn't put them in a garbage truck. Instead they would bury things in piles behind their house," she said. "And your yard would be the back of the blacksmith's house."

"So...?"

"So you might have a good chance of finding artifacts," she said. "If I were you, I'd get to work."

I rode my bike home as fast as I could. It took me only a few minutes to assemble my tools: string, a garden trowel, and an old school notebook. I carefully tied two pieces of string across the square to make a simple grid. I drew a picture of my grid and labeled the sections in my notebook: A, B, C, D.

When I came to the site the next day, I noticed that the gridlines had been moved. The dirt in Sector B looked disturbed. Someone had tampered with the site.

Figure 8–2.

"How's it coming, Gwen?" Mom asked. She walked across the yard to join me.

I reached into the freshly dug dirt and pulled out a small, shiny bone.

"Wow!" she exclaimed. "A bone! Maybe it belonged to a dinosaur."

"Perhaps," I said. "Or maybe it's a drumstick from the chicken we had for dinner last night."

"Some scientists think that birds are related to dinosaurs," Mom said hopefully, but then she sighed. "I couldn't fool you, could I?"

"Mom, I'm not five." I patiently told her why I had no chance of finding a real dinosaur bone in our backyard. "A dinosaur bone would be much farther down, and dinosaurs probably didn't live around here anyway. Besides, I want to be an archaeologist, not a paleontologist." I had learned this in my book. A paleontologist studies prehistoric animals, like dinosaurs. An archaeologist studies what people made.

Mom took the drumstick to the trash can. "I just didn't want you to be disappointed, honey," she said. "You might not find anything."

"I'm hopeful," I said. "By the way, can I have your colander?"

"My colander? I didn't know archaeologists made salad."

"I need it to screen the dirt," I explained. "I don't want to miss any tiny pieces of artifacts."

"I'll need to wash it first," Mom said. After half an hour she brought out the colander. "Do you need the can opener too?" she was about to joke, but she stopped when she saw what I was holding. "What's that?"

I turned the piece of pottery over in my hand. It didn't look like much—just a small, irregular chunk, covered in dirt. There was no chance that my mom had buried it—it was definitely old. When I scratched some of the dirt off with my fingernail, I could tell that it had once been white with blue specks.

"Congratulations, Gwen!" Mom exclaimed. "Well, I guess your work really paid off. Do you want me to put the shovel away for you?"

"Are you kidding?" I said. "Now the real work's just starting. I have to try to find more pieces. I have to figure out where they came from. Then I have to design the museum exhibit . . ."

"Museum?" echoed Mom.

I didn't let Mom see my work until after William came home. I have to admit that I felt a little jealous when I saw him lug home his crafts projects, camp pictures, and muddy shoes. He must have had a lot of fun.

But I had some work of my own to do. I spread my maps, posters, and diagrams on the dining room table. I made them close their eyes when they walked in.

"Oh, Gwen, this is marvelous," Mom said.

"You did all of this while I was gone?" William asked. He scratched at the poison ivy that covered his legs.

"Mom bought me a book about archaeology," I explained. "It was something fun to do while you were away, going on hikes and sleeping in tents."

"I didn't get to go on many hikes," he said, "and the tents were filled with spiders." He reached for my piece of pottery and examined it carefully. "Mom," he said, "maybe next summer, Gwen can go to camp, and I can stay home and do neat stuff like this."

William looked so disappointed that I forgot my jealousy. "Don't worry," I said. "There's plenty of archaeology for both of us. With your help, I can dig up the whole backyard!" I stole a quick glance at Mom, to see how she would react.

"I'm the one who bought you the book," she sighed. "Let's go see how many shovels we have. Gwen, I hope that you have room in your museum for more artifacts."

"We might need a bigger table," I said, and everyone laughed as we headed out, together, to see what else we could uncover.

FIGURE 8–2. *Continued*

> Sand box archaelogist is a book
> about a girl named Gwen who
> wants to be an archaeoliogist.
> After talking to her mom she
> starting Diging in the area of
> the old garden her mom puc a chiken
> Bone in the soil to test her
> daughter on her skills all Enou-
> gh She also did it to make sure
> She wouldn't be disipointed.

FIGURE 8–3. Sarah's Summary

in Corey's response (Figure 8–4). He included the main events, but he
did not see how the events add up to a theme. Also, the subplot about the
chicken bone does not really add to the conflict of the story, and can be
left out of a summary. Corey could use instruction in how to distinguish
between important and unimportant events, and how to look at those
events to find a theme.

> "Sandbox Archaeologist," is about
> a kid named Gwen. His brother, William,
> went to camp and Gwen got an
> archaeology book. He started to learn
> about archaeology and started digging.
> He found it very interesting. When
> Gwen thought he found something, it
> was just a chicken bone. Then
> he found a really old bone. He
> then thought he should start a museum.

FIGURE 8–4. Corey's Summary

Melissa's response shows some different characteristics (Figure 8–5). Melissa did a good job of stating the important events. She definitely understood the characters of the story, had an idea of the conflict, and even made a generalization in the last sentence. Many specific details were included, and the events were listed in order. She included character names and a statement of the conflict. Some of the paraphrasing is a little awkward, so she could benefit from instruction in restating ideas from the text.

Figure 8–6 is an example of a summary that deletes too many details and events. Dawn omitted the characters' names, which is not a good idea, and her summary did not reflect the ending of the story. It's impossible to

Gwen got an archaeolgy book while his older brother got to go to camp. Gwen though it was boring at first untill he got an Idea. He went to the libeary to see it the librain had old maps. she did and he whent home and started digging and found a piece of pottery then Willwam (older brother) came home and said "Next time Gwen can go to camp.". Gwen wasnt jelous anymore then.

FIGURE 8–5. Melissa's Summary

Reading Story

The story Sandbox Archaeology is about a little girl who's brother went to camp for the summer but her mother couldn't afford to send her. So she spent the summer Doing archaeology in her old garden.

FIGURE 8–6. Dawn's Summary

see inside a student's mind and know what she is thinking. Perhaps Dawn did not think that the narrator's name is important, or perhaps she did not infer the narrator's name. Regardless, she could benefit from some additional work on finding important events, identifying literary elements, and looking at story structure.

Tools for Narrative Summaries

Although I was reluctant to begin working with narrative summaries, I realized quickly that they are just as important for teaching and learning as expository summaries. In the next two chapters, you will find a collection of tools that I have used to help students improve their summaries of fiction. Through the use of story elements, retelling, and other activities, I have seen students write better summaries of narrative text . . . and firmly earned my official title of Summary Freak.

Chapter Summary

- Summarizing narrative text is considerably different from summarizing expository text, and requires different rules and different assessments.

- A good summary of narrative text includes important events, deletes trivia, accurately paraphrases the author's words, does not include irrelevant statements and opinions, and includes key story elements.

- To begin teaching narrative summaries, find out what your students can already do by asking them to read a story and write a summary.

9

USING STORY ELEMENTS TO IMPROVE NARRATIVE SUMMARIES

"And then the bomb exploded, right outside of the restaurant, and that guy that used to be the teacher jumped out, and we found that he"—

"No," Matt interrupted. "It wasn't the guy that used to be the teacher. It was the other guy, the one with the moustache."

Jorge made a face and continued without taking a breath. "And we found that he was the one who had been going all around, writing all the notes."

"There were notes?" I asked, perplexedly. "What were the notes?"

"The notes about the bombs!" Matt answered. "You forgot to tell her about that? That's like, the most important part. See, there were these notes. . . . "

One nice part of lunch duty is that it allows me time to talk with my students outside the classroom. Besides learning about how the dance went Friday night, favorite school lunch entrees, and who caused the second grade teacher the most grief, I also get to hear student reviews of the latest movies. These impromptu renditions are usually fast paced, exciting, and more than slightly flawed. But they are also a great way to find out what students already know about integrating the story elements into a summary.

Talking about a movie is just one reason to learn about summarizing fiction. For both the students and I, working with story elements is fun and intrinsically motivating. Through movies, short stories, books, and even pictures, we can help students find the key story elements and improve their summarizing.

Story Maps

An effective way to help students learn a process is to show an overview of the entire procedure and then go into more detail about each individual step. Because of this, I like to begin story elements instruction by working with students to create holistic story maps. Once students have the overall story structure in their heads, we can zoom in on individual story elements as needed.

The term *story map* can refer to a number of different graphic organizers. A story map can be as simple as a web with the conflict or theme in the middle, and events around the outside (Burns, Roe, and Ross 1996). In the intermediate grades, a story map is usually a more structured organizer with places for the student to write characters, setting, conflict, events, and theme. Whichever form of story map is used, it can help students to see the structure of the story as a whole.

Evidence suggests that throughout the intermediate grades, students improve in their abilities to recall structural elements of stories and use what they know about story structure to help them recall and comprehend stories (Fitzgerald, Spiegel, and Webb 1985). Working with a story map has proved to be an effective strategy to support students before, during, and after they read narrative text. Before reading, the story map can help to cue them to story elements to expect during their reading. During reading, the story map is a way for students to monitor their comprehension and keep track of the action in a story. After reading, the map requires students to reflect on what they read and make connections between story elements (Davis 1994). Explicit teaching of story structure, then, should have a positive impact on student summaries.

I use a fairly standard method for teaching story maps. We start by sharing a read-aloud text, chosen for its explicit use of story elements. Then, we complete a story map in chart form together. We talk about how to use the story map to write a summary. Many students are tempted to follow the formula, "The characters are_____. The setting is_____. The events are_____." Through group discussion, we find a better way to write the summary and post it on the chart. Finally, students work in groups to read other picture books, fill out story maps, and write summaries. These first summaries are often somewhat rough. Students are focused on including what is important and don't spend much time considering the best word choices or punctuation. However, the activity is valuable because it involves the students in a conversation about the literary elements. Through this conversation, they can learn from one another and refine their skills.

The story map can also be used to help students predict what will happen in the story. Distribute story maps to the students. Then, either read parts of the story aloud or copy quotes and hand them out to the students. As students read the story, they can compare their predictions with what actually happens.

Once I have used a simple story map with the entire class, I introduce the more complex story map (Figure 9–1) that I developed. Why did I make my own story map, when there are multitudes available in professional resources and online? I had several reasons, from theoretical to practical. Practically, I have found that giving students resources with lines provided leads to better work. (Someone should do a controlled research study to find out if this is true!) When students are faced with the simple webs with open spaces, they tend to scrawl in one- or two-word responses. With lines, though, I notice more thoughtful, detailed responses.

Theoretically, I wanted one story map that I could use all year long. My thinking was that if I used a consistent organizer, the students would transfer learning from previous texts to new tasks. Students could also keep and refer to past story maps to complete new ones. (Assuming they can find the previous papers!) I also thought that if I used a story map with the complex terms that they would be required to know later, they would learn the vocabulary more easily.

I was happy to see that this idea turned out to be a success. During our first attempt, we just filled in a few of the sections. Throughout the year, we added to the map. The students did become more competent as the year progressed. By the spring, some were even able to complete the story map and write a theme completely independently. We had made progress.

The story map, then, can help students to write a summary of the text. Whether they are able to fill out a few of the sections or whether they can move through the entire map, the resource cues them to think about the important part of a summary. It is an important scaffold to draw their attention to the critical parts of a story.

Just introducing the story map isn't always enough. Students often need more work with individual parts of the map. What can you do when students fill up all the lines for the events of the story and continue on to three more sheets of paper? What can you do when you are in a movie conversation, like the one with Matt and Jorge at the beginning of the chapter? These are problems with understanding and paraphrasing the plot events. There are several ways to deal with these problems.

Story Map

Title: _____ Author: _____

Genre: Realistic fiction   Historical fiction   Fantasy   Science fiction   Other

Characters

Major Character(s): The major characters are: _____

_____

Minor Characters: The minor characters are: _____

_____

Point of View

Check the point of view that the author uses:

_____3rd-Person (he/she/they; the narrator is not in the story)

_____Omniscient (all-knowing) narrator_____   Limited narrator_____

_____1st Person (I/me; the narrator is in the story)

Setting

General location _____   Time period _____

Check which type of setting is used:

_____Backdrop setting (setting not a major factor in the conflict or plot)

_____Integral setting (setting is essential to the story)

Explain your reasoning: I think the setting is _____

because _____

Conflict

Check the main type of conflict in the work:

___ character vs. man   ___ character vs. nature   ___ character vs. fate

___ character vs. society   ___ character vs. self

FIGURE 9–1.

Describe the conflict in several sentences. _____

_____

_____

_____

Plot

List the main events or complications in order:

a. The story begins with _____

_____

_____

b. The conflict develops when _____

_____

c. The climax (super event/big decision) happens when _____

_____

d. The main conflict is resolved when _____

_____

e. The story concludes with_____

_____

Theme

**Do not state theme in terms of plot.

Write the underlying message, or theme, of the story. _____

_____

Is this story worth reading? Why or why not? _____

_____

_____

FIGURE 9–1. *Continued*

Plot

Shrinking a story or book of many events into just a few short sentences can overwhelm many students. Plot is not simply the events in a story, but the entire underlying structure. A goal-based narrative begins with an exposition, which introduces the characters and setting; continues with the rising action, in which the conflict is introduced; reaches the point of highest tension with the conflict; and concludes with the falling action, in which the conflict is resolved.

Teaching Plot Parts

Keeping a poster of plot parts visible in my read-aloud area helps students to keep the overall plot structure in mind as we read. If students know how the plot parts correspond with story events, they can make decisions about which events are truly important. Events in the exposition, for example, are more about establishing characters and setting than developing the conflict, and can usually be omitted from a summary. The events in the climax, on the other hand, determine the outcome of the conflict. These events should always be included in a summary.

Because students need to see examples of how events correspond to plot parts, I model again and again. After my students read an excerpt from *Woodsong* by Gary Paulsen, I posted a large chart with a diagram of the plot structure. Then I handed out events from the story and asked students to match the events with the parts of the plot structure. After we put the events on the chart, we worked together to write a summary as a class. This helped students to see which events were critical to include in a summary and which were not.

Sequencing Plot Events

This activity takes some preparation time. It is helpful for students who have problems keeping plot events in sequence as they write.

1. Read the story carefully. Record all events, important or unimportant, on strips of paper. (I type mine into a table to save time.)

2. Scramble the events so that they are no longer in order.

3. Copy the page with the events and have students cut out each one. I make a transparency so that I can lead the activity on the overhead projector, but you could also rewrite the events on sentence strips.

4. With the students, decide which events are essential to the story and which can be eliminated. (Have extra strips available in case students think of collapsing lists and putting some events together.)

5. Arrange the events in order, showing the progression through the parts of the plot.

6. Have students use this list of events to write a summary, either individually or with a partner.

Text Features and Flashbacks

A flashback occurs when an author tells parts of the story out of order. How can readers deal with flashbacks when writing summaries? The first step is to help students identify flashbacks.

Although narrative texts don't include the same kinds of text features as expository texts, readers *can* learn from the physical layout of the text. Many novels will show a change of time or place through the use of blank lines or rows of asterisks. Some books use a different typeface to show a flashback or flashforward. Help students to become aware of these devices. When I started using *Holes* as a read-aloud selection, I photocopied pages and put them on an overhead transparency. Then, we talked about how the reader can tell when there is a change of time or place.

Identifying the flashback is just one step. How should these events, told out of sequence, be included in a summary?

Luckily, some flashback events can just be omitted. If a flashback is included simply to develop a character, and does not affect the outcome of the conflict, then the event can be left out of a summary.

When flashback events are an integral part to the conflict, the reader has a choice of whether to list the events in chronological order or to list them in the order in which they appear in the story.

Conflict

The conflict, or central problem, underlies all the action of a story. In literary terms, the conflict is the struggle between opposing forces. Students must be able to find the conflict to write a successful summary.

Classifying Conflict

Conflict exists in several forms. The classic kinds of conflict are *character versus character, character versus society, character versus fate, character versus himself,* and *character versus the environment.*

101

*Using Story
Elements
to Improve
Narrative
Summaries*

Students enjoy creating and acting out scenarios that depict a form of conflict. (Be careful with the character versus character conflicts, though!) This can be a kinesthetic activity for helping students learn story elements.

Look at what your students are reading to find other ways to teach these kinds of conflict. Students' independent reading books work well. One year, I found a different way, almost by accident. The boys in my class had recently discovered the irreverent humor of the comic strip *Calvin and Hobbes,* in which the unruly six-year-old Calvin and his stuffed tiger Hobbes wreak havoc at home, in school, and in the neighborhood. As I was planning a lesson about conflict, I happened to find a *Calvin and Hobbes* book that a student had left on the floor by my desk. Muttering about the irresponsibility of sixth graders, I picked it up to return to him. I glanced through it briefly before I set it on his desk. On one page, Calvin ponders the nature of humanity and the eventual outcome of events—a great example of a character-versus-fate conflict. On another page, Calvin and Hobbes (the stuffed tiger) are fighting. On yet another page, Calvin rails against the fact that he is forced to go to school. I quickly made transparencies of these pages to show to the students.

We then discussed the conflicts. Even a simple comic strip has layers of meaning, and different groups interpreted the conflict differently. "The one where they're fighting, that's character versus character," said Jessica.

Andrew disagreed. "But Hobbes is just a toy, so it's really Calvin versus himself." Looking around the room, I could actually see the moment of understanding as some students realized the deeper level of the text. By using what my students found interesting, I had helped them to understand conflict.

Movies can also help students get to a deeper level of understanding. There are so many instructional benefits to sharing a good movie with a class. A movie like *Sinbad: Legend of the Seven Seas* (2003) is both entertaining and multilayered. Sinbad, the protagonist, faces not only the evil goddess of chaos, but also an internal struggle of whether to save his friend or face certain death. Analyzing kinds of conflict can help students to find what is important in a story.

Verbs for Expressing Conflict

"The conflict is that Mrs. Frisby has to help her son."

"The problem is that the tractor will plow over Mrs. Frisby's house."

I wasn't happy with these awkward constructions that kept appearing in my students' summaries of *The Secret of NIMH*. The problem, I decided, was a lack of verbs. Students didn't have the language of literary discourse, and so they were expressing the ideas in the best way they could.

To help students break free of this pattern, I quickly jotted a list of verbs on an overhead transparency. After handing out dry-erase boards, I showed students the two problem sentences and the list of verbs (Figure 9–2). Next I asked students to rewrite one of the sentences with a verb from the list. Melanie wrote: *Mrs. Frisby faces a big problem. Her son Timothy is too sick to be moved and their house will be crushed when the farmer plows the field.* She had managed to replace her stilted sentence with some better writing, an improvement that carried through to her next summary. Teaching the verbs for conflict proved to be a simple and effective tool.

> **Warm-Up**
>
> Can you revise these sentences?
>
> Ⓐ The <u>conflict is</u> that Mrs. Frisby has to move her family before the farmer plows.
>
> Ⓑ The <u>problem is</u> that Mrs. Frisby's son will die if they don't move, but he is too sick to travel.
>
> Try these verbs:
> - faces   - challenges   - tries
> - encounters   - braves   - endeavors
> - opposes   - attempts

FIGURE 9–2. Warm-up

Characters

Who Is Important?

Not every character in a story is important. Cutting out the secondary characters can help students to manage a complex plot and keep their summaries brief.

Repeated references, a way of determining the topic of expository text, can also help students to find important characters. Characters who show up at many points throughout the story are usually important, whereas characters who appear only once or twice can be considered secondary.

Who's Telling This Story, Anyway?

When a story is told in first person, students often have trouble figuring out who is speaking. Teach them how to find the narrator of a story by looking for the character's name in dialogue, making guesses, and confirming predictions. Look at the example first person excerpt (Figure 9–3). Although *Amanda Sanders* is the first name mentioned, it is not necessarily the narrator's name. Not until the reader finds that the message over the intercom was meant for the narrator is her identity confirmed.

With some stories, you may just want to tell students the narrator's name. A literature anthology I used had an excellent chapter from *The Circuit* as one of the first selections. The narrator's name, Panchito, is given only once in the entire text. Instead of forcing students to scan the entire text and make this inference on their own, I told them the narrator's name,

---

My life went downhill sometime between seventh and eighth periods.

The loudspeaker to our classroom came on. "Excuse me, is Amanda Sanders there?"

My teacher paused in her droning and looked up toward the speaker, as if the person calling from the office could see her. "Yes she is," she answered, in a fake pleasant voice.

"Could you let her know that she is not to ride the bus home tonight? Her father will be picking her up."

"Certainly," Mrs. Spangler answered, and looked at me to make sure that I had gotten the message.

FIGURE 9–3. First Person Excerpt

and asked them to look for details to support whether Panchito was a boy or a girl. This gave them practice in finding details and confirming predictions without leading to frustration.

Standardized Test Help

During a practice standardized test, Carly raised her hand. I walked through the silent classroom to her desk. She pointed to a question. "It wants to know how Grady tried to convince his mother," she whispered. "But who is Grady? I can't find him in the story."

Luckily, this was just a practice session, so I was able to help Carly. I could see why she was having trouble. The story was told in first person and she had not made the connection that Grady was the narrator. "Did you read the introduction to the story?" I asked, pointing to the short blurb at the top of the page.

"No," she admitted, and read it to herself. The introduction set up the story, naming Grady as the narrator and outlining the problem. "Oh, I see. Thanks."

"Don't forget to read those extra parts," I told her. "You can usually find some good clues about the story."

First person narratives often appear on standardized tests, so Carly will probably encounter this kind of question again. I made a mental note to be more explicit with teaching students to use the text features of a test to help them comprehend the story.

Setting

Setting refers to the time and place of a story. Students are usually good at finding individual locations of a story—at school, in the barn, at the zoo—but have trouble generalizing their thinking.

Setting can be either *integral*, essential to the plot, or *backdrop*, not essential to the plot. In "Sandbox Archaeologist," the setting is just a backdrop. The story could take place in a variety of locations. Genres like historical fiction and science fiction, however, have integral settings. These settings are an important part of the story and must be reported in a summary.

Theme

During my first year of teaching reading, I labored to teach students about theme. It did not come easily for my students, who were used to thinking more concretely. In the midst of one particularly painful expla-

105
*Using Story
Elements
to Improve
Narrative
Summaries*

nation, a student asked, "Why do authors use theme, anyway? Why don't they just come right out and say what they mean?"

The answer? Because it would be dumb. Nobody likes to read the stories in which the author comes out and beats you about the head with a club called theme. It's more interesting when the theme is the subtle kernel at the heart of a well-told story, when days later, you are still thinking about what a story really means. Theme is not the moral of a story; instead, it is a comment or view on the nature of the world.

So we read picture books, watched movies, and listened to songs. We talked about themes and how the works would be different if the author stated the theme directly. Although students improved slightly, I was doomed to failure until I turned my thinking around.

I had been treating theme as deductive thinking, part to whole. Students had to take parts of the story and add them up to create a theme. This is difficult enough with expository text, but is even harder with narrative. How do I figure out themes? I realized that I have an internal library of themes that I page through when faced with a text—good will triumph over evil, persistence pays off, and so forth.

So I turned theme into an inductive process by giving the students a list of universal themes (Figure 9–4). Now they had the big idea and were trying to support their thinking with parts of the story. Every time they read another text, they added to their internal library of themes.

Don't be discouraged if students don't learn the concept of theme right away. When Kelsey came to me, in mid April, with her puzzled look and cute smile and her question, "What is theme, again?" I felt discouraged. I had taught students about theme on at least six different occasions. We had talked about theme in poetry, in novels, in short stories, even in songs. Students had copies of the universal themes and had discussed theme in their independent reading books throughout the year. Yet something had not clicked for Kelsey. Was I not trying hard enough?

As I delved into research on story elements, though, I discovered that maybe I was not such a bad teacher after all. Researchers have found that students need far more practice with the concept of theme than with other story elements. I wasn't doing anything wrong. In fact, by creating an environment in which we revisited the idea of theme over and over, I may have been doing something right. I shouldn't lament the fact that Kelsey didn't know what theme was in mid April—I should celebrate the fact that she was trying to find out.

Universal Themes

The theme of a text is an underlying message or comment on the world. In other words, it expresses what the author wants you to learn or think about after you read.

Many of the same themes are expressed over and over again in fiction. Some common themes are listed below. But this isn't a complete list!

Can you think of a movie, book, poem, or other work of literature that expresses one of these themes?

How we relate to each other
- Others may help us, but we must figure out who we really are on our own.
- Family is more important than popularity, wealth, etc.
- Sometimes we must go against what everyone else is doing and make our own path.
- A true friendship can withstand tests.
- Fighting doesn't solve problems.
-
-

How we relate to nature
- It is difficult for people from today's modern age to survive in the natural world.
- Nature is a healing force.
- People are destroying nature and humanity with uncontrolled technology.
-
-

Life in general
- Good can come from bad.
- Persistence and effort pay off in the end.
- Cheaters never win.
- Honesty is the best policy.
- There are more important things than money and success.
- Good will triumph over evil.

Growing up
- Growing up requires a person to make many difficult choices.
- Growing up is confusing.

FIGURE 9–4.

© 2006 by Emily Kissner from *Summarizing, Paraphrasing, and Retelling*. Portsmouth, NH: Heinemann.

Chapter Summary

107

*Using Story
Elements
to Improve
Narrative
Summaries*

- Teaching story elements will help students to understand and summarize narrative text.

- A story map is a useful tool to help students see the overall picture of a text.

- To help students understand plot, work with plot structure and finding important events.

- Teach students how to recognize when authors use flashbacks and flashforwards.

- Classifying types of conflict helps students to recognize conflict in stories.

- Teach verbs like *opposes, encounters,* and *faces* to help students write about conflict.

- Students sometimes have trouble deciding which characters in a story are important. Teach them to look for repeated references to primary characters.

- When a story is told in first person, a reader will have to read carefully to infer the name of the narrator. Don't assume that students already know how to do this!

- An integral setting should be named in the summary, whereas a backdrop setting can be omitted.

- Theme is a comment on the world or human nature. Giving students a list of universal themes helps them to assign themes to texts.

10 TALKING TO LEARN
Retelling in the Intermediate Classroom

I had always assumed that I would have a classroom filled with meaningful conversations, exciting discussions of children sharing knowledge. I had seen these kinds of classrooms and I knew it could be done.

But the grim realities of being a middle school teacher in an open space school dimmed my enthusiasm. We had 140 students in the five classrooms that made up our "suite," with only flexible walls separating us. On a good day you could hear five lessons going on at once. Whenever my students had conversations, the noise carried throughout all the adjacent rooms. Sometimes my students would not want to talk about the topic, sometimes they would talk too loudly, and I could always count on the fact that once they started talking, it was almost impossible to get them to stop.

As my classroom management skills increased, I began to allow some talking in the classroom, mostly during parts of the writing process. I worked to include talking and sharing as a prewriting activity. I structured peer conferences as a revising and editing strategy. Slowly, I gained confidence that I could allow students to have conversations and still maintain control of the class. But it wasn't until I left the open space school that I really discovered the power of conversation as a tool for helping students to summarize. And it took a kindergarten teacher to show me the true power of retelling.

Benefits of Retelling

How would you like a classroom activity that requires no paper grading, very little preparation time, and has a proven positive effect on student reading comprehension—even with minimal teacher feedback? Retelling is that amazing.

Basically, retelling is an oral activity in which students restate the main ideas or events of the text. Retelling is more than just simple recall.

Students must interact with the text, make decisions about what is important, and draw inferences to construct meaning through retelling.

Several studies have proved the benefits of retelling. A 1985 study showed that fourth graders who have engaged in retelling following a reading had remembered significantly more about a text than students who had been instructed to illustrate what they had learned. The students from the retelling group showed better immediate and delayed recall than the students from the illustration group (Gambrell et al. 1985). The gains from the retelling group even seemed to transfer to later readings.

A 1991 study showed that retelling can lead to impressive gains in reading comprehension for both proficient and less-proficient readers. Over four retelling sessions, the students' comprehension of the text improved, as well as their retellings. What makes this finding even more remarkable is that students in this study did not receive any explicit teacher instruction in retelling (Gambrel, Koskinen, and Kapius 1991).

Why is retelling so important? There are several reasons. Retelling can affect how much students learn by giving students a chance to add more information to their memory. By forcing a reader to restructure the text and reshape the concepts, retelling can also forge new links to information from the text. The verbal nature of retelling is also important. Somehow, talking about a text may help a reader to shape comprehension and understandings.

Pretelling

The kindergarten year is an amazing one. The raw recruits come into class barely knowing how to write their names. There is no class dynamic, little understanding of what it means to function as a group, and no idea of how to get along in the school culture. By May, a kindergarten class is a swarming hive of organized activity. Students know how to follow routines—how to sign in, how to go to centers, what to do at lunchtime, and all the other little tasks that make up a day of school.

I have great respect for the patience of the kindergarten and first grade teachers who start this process. It might seem like these routines are just practicalities to help the day along and make the most efficient use of time. However, it turns out that they are the foundation for the summarizing we expect of our upper grade students.

I first learned about pretelling from my son's kindergarten teacher, Christine McGough. The kindergarten team had been studying the book *The Power of Retelling* by Vicki Benson and Carrice Cummins (2000).

According to this book, pretelling is an important step in the developmental process to retelling and then to summarizing. Before students can tell a story with a beginning, middle, and end, they need to experience the concepts of beginning, middle, and end over and over again.

The pretelling process is quite simple. Before students begin a routine, the teacher works with them to make a list of the steps they will do. Then they do the activity, such as getting ready for lunch, selecting books, or completing an art project. After the process is over, the class reflects on what actually happened and go over the steps one more time. Ordinary activities like signing in for lunch become instructional activities. Zachary and Mrs. McGough recalled the pretelling process they used for putting on winter clothes.

"Do you remember that we put on the mittens first?" Mrs. McGough asked. "Did that work very well?"

Zachary shook his head. "It was hard to put on our coats."

"So then we went back to the steps, and changed them around," Mrs. McGough said. Something so simple as putting on winter clothing had become a rich conversation to help students think sequentially. During the remainder of the year, the kindergarten class went through more stages of developmental retelling, including shared and guided retellings (Benson and Cummins 2000).

My students were beyond simple pretelling activities like these. Sixth graders would not take kindly to writing down the steps to putting on winter clothes before recess—I have trouble convincing some of them even to wear a coat. With some alterations, though, the technique had promise. My students could identify steps in a process, but they were still not adept at showing causal links and elaborating with details. Could I adapt pretelling to help students do this?

I tried it with a transition visit to the middle school. My sixth graders were about to leave elementary school for the middle school, and we had a scheduled trip so that the students could see where they were to go. Shortly before we boarded the buses, students and I made a list of things that they thought would happen and feelings they thought they would have. Because the middle school principal and guidance counselor had visited the previous day, students had some ideas.

"We'll see Mr. Zinn!" "Have slushies in the cafeteria!" "We'll get shoved in lockers!" "It will be exciting." "We'll see inside our classrooms."

Then we put the list aside and went ahead with the activity. After we returned, we looked back to what we thought would happen, then added or changed events. "We didn't really get to see in the classrooms—we just walked by," Jennifer said.

"But we did get slushies," Brooke said.

"I thought it would be exciting, but I was kind of bored," Jacob commented, to a chorus of disagreement from other students.

After this, students turned to a partner to retell the events of the day. Not only were their retellings filled with the important events, but students also elaborated with some of their thoughts and feelings.

A few weeks later, I added some more elements to the pretelling scenario. Here was my thinking. Pretelling is useful because students develop concrete experiences with beginning, middle, and end. Could I give my students concrete experience with the summarizing tasks they find challenging—deleting trivia and including main ideas? It was worth a try.

We were about to go to the Kids' Inquiry Conference, or KIC, a children's science conference held at a nearby university. Before we went, we wrote about our expectations, as before. I made a chart for students to record their predictions.

Several days after we returned, we reflected on our trip. Students began by sharing their expectations and talking about whether they were true or false. Then they took turns retelling the events of the day to a partner. Because everyone had chosen different sessions, we learned a lot from listening to each other. We made an overall listing of events on the chalkboard. Most of the events were what I expected—arriving, learning about the structure of the day, going to sessions, and enjoying the hands-on area. But I found out that even the most carefully planned trips sometimes hold an element of surprise.

"And then, at lunchtime, we went to the café to eat," Melissa said.

I nearly dropped the chalk. I had eaten my meager packed lunch on a bench outside. "There was a café?"

Other students nodded. "My grandmother took us," Melissa added.

"They had good cheeseburgers," Jeremy put in.

"Oh, and Jared was eating out of the trash can," Jorge said.

"They were just cheese curls!" Jared protested. "And they were still in the wrapper."

This was a great teachable moment. Just as kindergarteners need to experience beginning, middle, and end, my sixth graders could experience deleting trivial details. I hastily jotted down all that they said.

"If we were going to write a summary of the day for Mrs. Daugherty (our principal), which events would be important?" I asked. "And which ones would be trivial details that we can eliminate?"

"Include the cheese curls! Include the cheese curls!" some students said, because sixth graders are at the age where they will say just about anything for a laugh.

Brooke raised her hand. "The details about the cheese curls and the café are interesting, but I don't think they're important," she said.

This was just the kind of thinking that I was looking for. In reading, students have trouble differentiating between what is important and what is interesting. One key to helping them make this distinction is by helping them to see the difference in real-life events.

After finding the most important events, we managed to condense all the events of the day into six sentences. The entire lesson reinforced for me that intermediate students benefit from concrete experiences just as much as kindergarteners do. Retelling an event like this can add an instructional component to almost any activity. Too often, I overlook the connections that I could make between the curriculum and those activities that I think of as "extra." However, as Mrs. McGough showed, there can be considerable learning in these incidental moments—even for sixth graders.

Retelling Directions

"I don't get it."

How many times have you heard those words? After carefully crafting directions, discussing them in class, and asking for any questions, I cringe when I hear those words. Do I really have to explain the whole thing again?

There are many ways to end the "I don't get it" virus, and retelling is one of them. When discussing a set of lengthy instructions—to a math game, for instance—give students a period of time to read the directions, and then tell them to turn to a partner and retell what they read. As partners compare their retellings, they often hear inaccuracies or notice gaps in their understanding. This gives them a real, authentic reason to go back to the text. A teacher can easily tell which parts of the directions were easy to understand, and help clarify those parts that may be problematic.

Retelling and Read-Aloud

Read-aloud is an important part of my language arts routine. It is an important shared activity for our class and helps give us a common experience to talk about.

Wiggly, social middle school students, however, can prove to be a challenging audience. Retelling is a way to focus their attention and keep them engaged in the read-aloud. To build movement into our class time, I conduct read-aloud sessions on the floor in the back of the classroom. This gives the students a much-needed change of venue. When they arrive, sometimes I say, "Turn to the person beside you and retell yesterday's chapter."

Retelling is also important during and after the reading. As students become comfortable with retelling, call on volunteers to retell what they heard so far. After students have become competent retellers, call on someone at random to retell a chapter. (I put student names on Popsicle sticks and draw them out of a cup . . . very suspenseful!) Because students don't know if their names will be called, they are more motivated to stay alert and thinking throughout the session.

Retelling Reading Selections

Retelling is also a tool for reading comprehension. Giving students time to retell what they have read has benefits for both the reteller and the listener. The reteller can experience the reorganization of information that accompanies talking through a text; the listener can hear another perspective on a shared reading. Even better, the teacher can listen in on a few retellings to gauge quickly how well students in the class understood the text.

Retelling can be used in several ways. To bridge selections read over several days, you can use retelling as a lesson opener. You can have students read short segments of a text and retell at regular intervals. Retelling can also be a tool to keep students focused during a long reading selection. To keep the sessions under control, think about these factors.

1. What directions will be given?

   a. Put directions on the board or an overhead transparency so students can clearly see what to do. Be sure that they are familiar with what a retelling is before you begin. If they do not know the term, model a brief retelling for them.

2. How will students be paired?

   a. Sometimes I pair up the students, and sometimes I allow them to choose their partners. When I have my desks set up in a table arrangement, it is easy for students simply to turn to the person sitting beside them. When students have to move, I set the timer to give them a minute to get settled in a new place.

   b. If you have a short selection, each partner can retell. Break up longer selections into chunks and have students alternate retelling and listening.

3. How will students get feedback?

   a. Feedback is not absolutely necessary for retelling to be effective. But I find it useful to have students complete a quick rating sheet. For a fiction retelling, they can check off as the other student names the story elements; for a nonfiction retelling, they can mark a box as their partner states the main ideas. (I never assign grades based on the student feedback, however, because I can't trust the validity of the peer response.) They treat the task as more worthwhile if they have paperwork to do! In an ideal world, I would always have a neat stack of retelling forms ready for students to complete. However, this isn't a perfect world. There's no shame in showing an overhead transparency of a simple rating scheme, and having students copy the ratings on their own sheets of notebook paper.

I had always assumed that retelling belonged in the primary grades. However, retelling has a definite place in the intermediate classroom. Through retellings of events, students can experience some of the key skills for summarizing.

Chapter Summary

- Retelling is an oral activity in which readers retell what they remember of a text.

- Even without teacher feedback, retelling has been shown to impact comprehension positively.

- Pretelling of events can help students to make links between events and understand chronological order.

- Retelling can help structure read-aloud sessions.

- Before starting retelling in the classroom, think about how you will structure the session, pair the students, and provide for feedback.

11

SCAFFOLDING FOR SUMMARIZING

Same grade, different worlds—that is what it felt like when I moved from teaching sixth grade in a middle school to teaching sixth grade in an elementary school. Besides suddenly being responsible for teaching all the subject areas instead of just language arts, I also had to deal with recess, dispensing fluoride tablets, and walking the students around the building. I felt silly as I lined them up like ducklings to walk to lunch! As the year wore on, I began to enjoy moving through the hallways with the students. Waiting by the water fountain for everyone to get drinks, I had a good opportunity to talk with students.

"What are we doing when we get back to class, Mrs. Kissner?" Brendan asked me one afternoon.

"Well, I thought that I might teach you a code," I answered.

A few of the other kids, overhearing the conversation, murmured approval. "Cool," Brendan said. "What kind of code?"

"It has these funny marks on a page, and if you put them together in the right way, these marks can tell stories," I answered.

Brittney and Liz figured it out and grinned at me. "I think I've seen this code before," Andrea said with a groan, and the other students started laughing as they figured out what I was talking about. We headed back to the classroom and settled into our language arts routine. Somewhere between read-aloud and writing time, Matt looked up and said, "Hey, what about that code you said you'd teach us?"

When you consider the act of reading, it really is a miraculous thing. A reader looks at the funny marks on the page, figures out the words they represent, and puts those words together to make sentences, paragraphs, and stories. The goal of reading is to make sense of these little squiggles, for those words to go into our brains and interact with what is already there and create an understanding that is entirely new. This is reading comprehension.

Reading comprehension has two levels: literal comprehension, or understanding what is directly stated by the author, and higher order comprehension, which goes beyond the literal meaning of the text and requires students to make interpretations and analyze information (Burns et al. 1996). Matt's remark showed that he had a literal understanding of what I was saying about a code, but he did not make the higher order connection that I was really talking about reading.

As reading teachers, we want to help students make meaning of what they read at both levels. We do this by thinking about strategies for students to use before reading, strategies for students to use during reading, and strategies to use after reading. Summarizing, paraphrasing, and retelling are ideal to use during and after reading strategies. Not only will students be able to monitor their own comprehension better, but they will also be required to think about the text on multiple levels.

At the literal level, summarizing requires students to think about what is important in the text and what main ideas are stated. At the higher order level, summarizing helps students to condense, generalize, and make inferences from the text. Students are forced to make choices about what is most important, and decide what could be stated in similar but slightly different ways. It just makes sense to build experiences with retelling and summarizing into everyday routines.

A wonderful feedback loop develops. Take time to teach students about summarizing and the skills needed to write good summaries. Then, use these skills as tools for helping students to understand text. Taking time to summarize improves students' reading comprehension, which then improves their summarizing ability. The benefits go on and on.

Does teaching about summarizing throughout the school year sound boring? Actually, it can be quite interesting. Summarizing becomes a tool for reading instead of the topic of learning. The goal is not to learn about summarizing; the goal is to use summarizing as a tool for learning. But using summarizing as a comprehension tool requires more than just telling kids, "Go summarize." Students need thoughtful scaffolding to help them understand how summarizing, retelling, and paraphrasing can help them understand what they read.

Scaffolding is a support for students as they complete a task that they could not accomplish on their own. There are several approaches you can take to build scaffolds for reading comprehension, including moment-by-moment verbal scaffolding and creating instructional frameworks (Clark and Graves 2005). These approaches can be used on a day-to-day basis to help students use summarizing to improve reading comprehension.

Moment-by-Moment Verbal Scaffolding

When I think about the moments when I really feel that I have been an effective teacher, I don't picture myself filling out report cards or writing on the chalkboard. I think of the times when I have worked directly with a student to solve a problem or answer a question. There is a magic in that moment when a teacher works individually with a student at the point of need.

This is moment-by-moment verbal scaffolding. When students encounter a problem in their reading, the teacher is there with questions and prompts that guide the student to solve the problem. What student wouldn't benefit from instant assistance and feedback? Moment-by-moment scaffolding is immediate, individualized instruction.

Unfortunately, many intermediate teachers feel that they don't have time to work individually with students. There have been days when I feared that if I stopped to talk individually with a student, the rest of the class would careen completely out of control. And when I worked in a schedule with forty-minute classes, a three-minute conversation with one student took up a big chunk of instructional time. When a child came to me with a question, I didn't know how to find out quickly where comprehension had broken down. And I really had no idea of what was going on inside the heads of the students who didn't come to me with questions.

Prompting students to summarize, paraphrase, and retell parts of a text has helped me to provide more individualized scaffolding, even in the context of large classes and short periods. Using what I know about the nature of summarizing has enabled me to support students as they try to solve their comprehension problems. For the students who don't ask questions, I use retelling to assess their comprehension quickly and decide whether I need to provide more individual support.

Here is an example of how this can work. In science class, I often plan "inquiry periods" during which students can use all the classroom resources to investigate their own questions. Not only does this build student interest in science, but it also improves literacy skills. Students comb books of science experiments to find projects to try, record their discoveries to share with other students, and use reference books to try to explain their results (Pearce 1999).

This time can be very chaotic, because students are scattered all over the room, engaged in their own projects. My name echoes as students call me over to see what they have done or ask for more supplies. The atmosphere doesn't seem like a place for one-on-one reading instruction, but the opposite is true. When students ask me to clarify or explain ideas in texts, they have a strong motivation to comprehend what they are reading. They are not just going through the motions to read a text that I have assigned. Instead, they are excited to comprehend a text that has personal meaning for them. I remember how the inquiry period taught Liz and Andrea an important lesson about reading directions.

"What have you girls created?" I asked, raising my eyebrows at the plastic cup filled with a mix of newspaper and water.

They looked at each other and laughed. "We were trying to make paper mash," Liz said. "We could use it to make sculptures and shapes."

"But we were supposed to let it soak overnight," Andrea continued. She regarded the mixture ruefully. "We didn't read the entire set of directions first."

Science allows students to internalize the reading strategies I have been trying so hard to teach. I could tell students a thousand times to read all directions before starting an activity; firsthand experience convinced them.

One day I looked up from watching a group of boys measure the power of a battery-operated water pump to find Tara at my elbow. Tara had found a pebble with what looked like bite marks in it a few days before, and had been intrigued with fossils ever since. Earlier in the week, I had found an online video about fossils for her to watch, and now she was ready to follow a set of directions to make a model fossil of her own.

The directions, though, were giving her trouble. I have science books of all reading levels, and she had one that was beyond her reach. Tara is a learning support student and has trouble with chunking and decoding longer words. The motivation to read was there, but the comprehension was not.

"Open your journal," I told Tara. (All the students had made small science journals they could use to record their research, findings, and conclusions.) "I'm going to read each step to you, and then we're going to work together to put it in your own words. Then, I'll write it down for you in your journal."

I decided upon this course of action for several reasons. My goal for Tara was for her to be able to paraphrase, or put a set of procedures into her own words. Right now, her problems with decoding were keeping her from doing this. If I just left her to puzzle through on her own, she might become frustrated with the entire process and give up. I chose to write down the steps for her so that she would have a clear, easy-to-read set of steps, and so that she could focus on the paraphrasing rather than writing.

During the next few minutes I read the steps aloud to her. With some help, she was able to put each step into her own words. I wrote down the steps in her journal and went back over the procedure with her. Later, she could follow the steps to complete the procedure. The scaffolding had helped her to take a difficult text, put it in her own words, and do an activity that she was motivated to complete.

But what about the students who don't come and ask questions? Intermediate-level students often do not self-check to see if they have understood a passage or not. Many of my students just want to get to the end of a text and say, "I'm done." How can I help them to use metacognitive strategies to see if they have learned from a text?

By prompting students to paraphrase or summarize a selection, I can lead them to see the gaps in their understanding. This is a quick way to do some individual scaffolding. An example is when Dennis was reading *Westward to Home: Joshua's Diary, The Oregon Trail, 1848 (My America)* (Hermes 2001), I had been talking with him about the book and reading his responses on his independent reading assignments, so I had an idea of where he was in the book. "What has happened in this chapter, Dennis?" I asked, as I walked by his desk during independent reading time.

"They have started on the Oregon Trail," Dennis answered. "They have their wagons and their supplies."

I thought back to my previous conversation with Dennis. This sounded very much like what he said before. "Didn't that happen back in the beginning of the book?" I asked. "Has anything happened since?" Looking over his shoulder, I could see that he was on page eighty-seven—definitely far enough for him to have read more events.

"Well . . . " Dennis said, doubtfully. "I guess so."

Many intermediate students remember a few key events from the beginning of a book and do not pay attention to important ideas later on in the book. They do not know to stop at intervals throughout the book and think about what has already happened. Prompting students to retell parts of the story is the scaffold for them to become more reflective.

I leaned down beside Dennis and showed him how to go back through what he had read and skim for the important events. "I'll be back in about five minutes," I told him. "I want to hear some more important events that have happened."

As students become more adept at a skill, the teacher slowly removes the support of the scaffolding. I considered this as I returned to talk to Dennis.

"They had to cross a river that had a flood," Dennis told me when I returned to his desk. "And one man fell into the river and got hurt."

"That sounds like something important," I told him. "Good job. Here is a sticky note. I'd like you to put it at the end of the next chapter to remind you to stop and think about what has happened." The sticky note would be a reminder for him to stop and summarize his reading, a visual cue for him to monitor his comprehension.

Individual scaffolding is a wonderful way to help students develop self-monitoring skills. However, there are not enough minutes in the day to meet individually with every child. Sometimes we need a strategy that works with a whole class of students. This is where instructional frameworks are useful.

Scaffolding with Instructional Frameworks

An instructional framework is a procedure that helps students navigate their way through a text. Instructional frameworks abound in the professional literature—directed reading–thinking activity, Re-Quest, reciprocal teaching, and so forth (Vacca and Vacca 2002). Every instructional framework is a tool for structuring a lesson. As I worked with summarizing, paraphrasing, and retelling in my classroom, I created two instructional frameworks of my own to help guide reading comprehension.

Steps for Summarizing

Don't let the term *instructional framework* frighten you. A useful framework doesn't have to be fifteen pages long and require intensive student training. This is quick and simple!

Students often read different articles, stories, and books. I want them to practice summarizing, but I don't just want to let them loose. I created the steps for summarizing sheet (Figure 11–1). By leading students to think about the main ideas, key words, and author's purpose of a text, this sheet provides the scaffolding for students to write a good summary.

Before students use this activity independently, I model the structure during a reading lesson. I make an overhead transparency of a text and work with the students to find main ideas, identify the author's purpose, and list key words. Together, we create a summary that we post in the classroom.

Steps for Summarizing Expository Text
Student Guide Sheet

- Carefully read the text. Remember to look at text features to help you find main ideas and important information. Write notes about main ideas below.

> [blank box]

- Think about key words from the article. List a few key words below. These words should be included in your summary.

> _____

- Think about the author's purpose. In other words, why did the author write the text?

    to inform   **to persuade**   **to entertain**

- Write your summary on the lines below. Remember:
  - Delete trivia
  - Delete repeated information
  - Collapse lists
  - Choose or create a topic sentence

> [blank lines]

- Read over your summary. Check to make sure that it includes the important information. Remember, do not include your own opinion—only the opinion of the author!

- Rate your summary.

    Excellent   **Good**   **Fair**   **Poor**

FIGURE 11–1.

After the shared experience, students use the framework on their own. The rating scale at the bottom is especially helpful, because it allows me to see if there is a match between the students' meta-cognition and their performance. A student who rates her summary as "Excellent" but does not include the main idea of a text is not monitoring her comprehension effectively.

As I have used this sheet, I have found that some students will skip over the vocabulary section at the top. They do not write key words from the article, and their summaries are usually quite poor. Students who pay attention to the features of the framework can produce reasonably good summaries. By following these steps again and again, students internalize the requirements of a good summary and become more skilled.

Main Idea Groups

The idea for main idea groups grew out of a strategy used by my father, Charles Pearce, to run student discussion groups.

"I don't have leaders that are strong enough," I complained. "I set aside time for discussion groups, and they either all talk about the wrong things or no one talks at all."

"Ah," said my dad. "Have you thought about using a script?"

A script? "Aren't they supposed to be discussing?" I asked. "How would a script help?"

That was when he showed me his procedures for SDQ, or student-developed questioning. The idea is simple. Before the group meeting, students develop questions about a text. During the meeting, a student leader follows a script to lead the discussion and keep everyone on track. Students ask and answer their own questions about a text. It is a great way to get meaningful discussions started.

The script works especially well for intermediate learners who are working hard for the approval of their peers. To a twelve-year-old, leading a reading discussion can seem, well, dorky. Not many middle school students would willingly say, "Can you provide text evidence for your thinking?" to their peers. The script relieves them of worrying what the other students will think of them. They become free to share their ideas and lead the group effectively.

I adapted SDQ for several uses in my own classroom, including the main idea groups. I developed the main idea groups in order to have a procedure for students to read articles about topics that interest them, and then meet in groups to discuss these articles. I also wanted a way to keep students thinking about the skills for summarizing. After all, students will only remember what is continually reviewed. Participating in the Main Idea Group procedure keeps the ideas of text structure, author's purpose, and main idea fresh in students' minds.

Students begin by reading the selected text and completing the Main Idea Group Preparation Sheet (Figure 11–2). This focuses their thinking on text structure and main ideas. Then they attend the group meeting in the designated place. The leader reads from the Main Idea Group Leader Guidelines (Figure 11–3) to keep the discussion going. There is a beauty to standing in the middle of the classroom and hearing four discussion groups going on all around! After the discussion, students use the main idea statements and important details to write a summary of the text.

I made a few other adjustments to the original structure of the groups, including adding the job of monitor. The monitor uses the Group Accountability Form (Figure 11–4) to list whether group members are prepared for the session and tally on-task and off-task comments. Because I can't be in every group, I depend on the monitors to tell me how each discussion went.

The best group leaders are often the most social students in the class. These students are not necessarily the best readers or most committed students. Placing them in a position of responsibility and control is very motivating for them. Even some of the most disruptive students function well when they lead a group.

Life in an intermediate classroom is never dull. I originally only had a column for on-task comments and off-task comments. During a session with a particularly difficult class, I was called over to mediate a dispute between a monitor and a group member.

"Heidi marked me down for an inappropriate comment, but I didn't say anything," Danny complained.

"You were throwing eraser bits at me!" Heidi retorted.

I looked at Danny to see if this was true. "Yeah, but I didn't make an inappropriate comment!" he grinned.

I sighed. "Write down exactly what Danny was doing on your record sheet," I told Heidi. When it came time to have group meetings again, I made sure that I included a new column for the monitor to record instances of inappropriate behavior.

Main Idea Group Preparation Sheet

Directions: Complete the sheet below, **before** you attend your group meeting.

Title of the text_____

Topic of the text_____

I think that the author's purpose is

to inform	to persuade	to entertain

I think that the text structure is

- Description/listing
- Compare and contrast
- Problem/solution
- Cause and effect
- Chronological order

Clue words that helped me to find the text structure: _____

_____

_____

Write a sentence to express the main idea of the text.

_____

_____

_____

Below, list 3–5 other important ideas from the text.

- _____
- _____
- _____
- _____
- _____

FIGURE 11–2.

Main Idea Group Leader Guidelines

Begin by checking attendance in the group. Remind the monitor to record the names of the students in the group **and** whether everyone brought the necessary materials to the meeting.

Say: Can anyone tell the topic of the selection?
Choose a student to share their summary of the story. Discuss.

Say: Can anyone tell the author's purpose?
Choose a student to share their response. Discuss.

Say: Now it's time to share our main ideas. Who would like to start?
Choose a student to share the main idea. Continue so that everyone shares.

Say: What do our main idea statements have in common?
Choose student to share answers. Discuss.

Say: Which main idea statement is best for the text?
Choose students to share their thoughts. Discuss as needed. If students disagree, tell them to go back to the text for evidence to support their points of view.

Say: Can anyone share another important idea from the text?
Choose a student to share another important idea.

Say: Does everyone agree that that is an important idea?
Choose students to discuss. Repeat sharing important ideas until the group decides that all important ideas have been discussed.

Say: Let's sum up what we talked about today. We read _____ and decided that the topic was _____. The author's purpose was to _____, and the main idea was _____. Does everyone agree?
Discuss.

Say: Let's complete the pluses and deltas for our meeting today. Does anyone have a comment to share?
Choose students to share. The monitor should record.

Say: Thank you for attending this group meeting. Please return to your seats to complete the summary of the text. When you are finished, please give your summary and preparation sheet to the monitor.

Thank you for your hard work in being a group leader!

FIGURE 11–3.

Group Accountability Form

While your group meets, keep track of student performance using the form below.

Selection title _____ Date of meeting _____

Student name	Prepared for meeting? Yes or No	On-task comments	Off-task comments	Inappropriate behavior
Group leader	To be prepared, students need a completed Prep. Sheet and the reading selection	Make a tally for every on-task comment a student makes	Make a tally for every off-task comment a student makes	Make a tally for every instance of inappropriate behavior
Monitor				

Group meeting debriefing

What went well in your group meeting?	What would you change for next time?

FIGURE 11–4.

The main idea group is an opportunity for students of mixed abilities to get together to share their thinking about main ideas. By listening to one another explain and defend their choices of main ideas, students get new insights into summarizing. The leader's script guides students to return to the text to seek evidence to support their ideas. This is an instructional framework that supports students as they develop their summarizing skills.

Chapter Summary

- Summarizing, paraphrasing, and retelling are ways to build scaffolds for students to help them improve their reading comprehension.

- With moment-by-moment verbal scaffolding, the teacher provides immediate guidance and feedback at the point of need.

- Instructional frameworks like main idea groups and steps for summarizing are other ways to scaffold for students.

SUMMARIZING FOR THE CONTENT AREAS 12

As students begin their educational careers, summarizing and retelling are useful tools to help them improve as readers. After children reach the intermediate grades, where they are expected to learn and remember content, summarizing becomes equally important for helping students to remember important ideas.

Secondary teachers are familiar with the difficulties that students face with content area textbooks. It is estimated that 75 percent of students have trouble reading science textbooks (Carnine and Carnine 2004). I had firsthand experience with this problem during a graduate class, when we used readability formulas to calculate the reading levels of the textbooks our students used. The sixth grade science text turned out to be written at the ninth grade level. Obviously, our students would have trouble reading and learning from these texts.

If students were motivated to read and learn from textbooks, they might be able to overcome the reading-level difficulties. But the content presented in textbooks does not always grab a reader's attention. When adults rated ideas from texts for "interestingness" and importance, practically none of the important ideas from an expository text were considered interesting (Hidi, Baird, and Hildyard 1982). Many of today's textbooks are filled with pictures, charts, and interesting little anecdotes. When well chosen, these text features can add to the meaning of the text and help readers stay interested. However, when the sidebars and other features are only slightly related to the text, they may impair comprehension. Both seventh grade and adult readers have significant difficulty in recalling main ideas when they read a text filled with "seductive details," the interesting little bits that do not contribute to the overall meaning of the text (Garner et al. 1989). So a little sidebar that tells an interesting story may actually keep students from finding the main ideas on the rest of the page.

Because students have difficulty learning from textbooks, teachers often explain important concepts during lectures. This introduces a new set of problems. How will students remember the important ideas from the presentation? How can a teacher help students learn the content?

Summarizing, paraphrasing, and retelling are useful in content area classes. Not only do these processes help students to comprehend text, they also help students remember new ideas. Whether you are helping third graders learn about kinds of trees or ninth graders learn about the Bill of Rights, summarizing can be a very beneficial tool.

Summarizing and Brain Research

Try this for an eye-opening activity. On any given day, follow your students around, from class to class, and do what they do. You will probably be amazed by all the information that is presented. In math, science, social studies, health class, and beyond, students are constantly seeing new vocabulary, new ideas, and new concepts.

How does the information from the chalkboard make it into a student's long-term memory? Learners will only remember information that makes sense and has meaning (Sousa 2001). This is true for adults as well as students. You may have sat through an inservice presentation about a subject you do not teach. Even though what you heard made sense, you probably didn't remember it all because the information had little meaning for you.

When I was teaching about chemistry and simple reactions, I consulted one of my husband's old college textbooks for information about acids and bases. What I read had meaning to me, but I didn't have enough of a chemistry background to understand it. The information did not make sense and I did not remember it the next day.

Sense and meaning are not all that is needed for students to remember information. Rehearsal is another vital process. When I need to remember a phone number, I repeat it over and over again. This is a form of rehearsal called *rote rehearsal*. The phone number will only make sense if it is remembered in the exact order that I learned it.

Most of what our students learn in a day, however, does not need to be remembered exactly as it is presented. Instead of rote rehearsal, this information is best learned through *elaborative rehearsal*. Elaborative rehearsal involves thinking back over information, making connections, and considering relationships.

We all want our students to learn information. Summarizing, paraphrasing, and retelling are ways for students to attach sense and meaning to information and to engage in elaborative rehearsal.

Asking students to *retell* a text not only enhances their comprehension of that text, but also increases the likelihood that they will remember information from that selection. It provides students with a chance to go back through the reading and attach sense and meaning to what they have read.

Through *paraphrasing*, students put ideas from a text or lecture in their own words. This is a form of elaborative rehearsal. To restate the important information in their own words, students need to consider relationships and connections among concepts.

Summarizing, like retelling and paraphrasing, is another powerful way to help students attach sense and meaning to what they have learned. During a short science lecture, I stop at predetermined intervals for students to write a quick summary of what they have heard so far. Circulating around the room and looking at student summaries allows me to see what students have understood well and whether I need to make the main ideas more clear. For students, writing the summary helps them to make sense of what they have heard and to organize their thinking.

I use this strategy with videos as well. My students love to watch *Bill Nye the Science Guy*, a series of great science programs. To keep them from being just passive observers, I stop the tape several times during the show and tell students to jot down a quick summary of the preceding section.

Retelling, paraphrasing, and summarizing lectures and videos are ways to help students learn content area knowledge. How can we help students cope with difficult textbooks and reading selections?

Concept Mapping and Summarizing

Difficult text structures abound in content area reading texts. Social studies articles may be written in cause-and-effect order, a math textbook may use chronological order to show how to solve a problem, a science trade book may use compare-and-contrast order to show the differences between insects and arachnids. How can students make sense of it all? Concept mapping is a way to help students see the connections between ideas before they write a summary.

A concept map is any kind of graphic organizer that visually shows relationships between ideas. A map can be created to represent any kind of text structure. I've had students use tree maps for text in main idea order, Venn diagrams for comparing and contrasting, sequence chains for items in chronological order, and so forth. Maps are effective because they show students a variety of ways to express ideas, and they help students to see what is important in a text.

On its own, concept mapping is a good way to help students comprehend a text. When paired with summarizing, concept mapping becomes even more valuable. When college students were asked to make concept maps before writing a summary, their summaries improved. Not only did students seem to understand text written better in the less familiar text structures like problem–solution, they also included more transition and connecting words in their summaries, showing that they noticed more connections between concepts (Ruddell and Boyle 1989).

I like concept mapping because it's easy to implement. This year, I taught sixth graders how to make tree maps to take notes on a science article (Figure 12–1). The first step was helping students set up the maps. It may seem tempting to make a frame of the concept map and hand it out so that students can fill it in. I've noticed that this only leads students to go on an answer hunt instead of reading the text. Instead, I use the overhead projector to show what the map looks like. Students need some very specific directions at first. The conversation ends up sounding something like this: "Turn your paper so you are holding it sideways, landscape style. Yes, I guess you could call it hot dog style also. Andrew, are you paying attention? This way you will have enough room to set up your map.

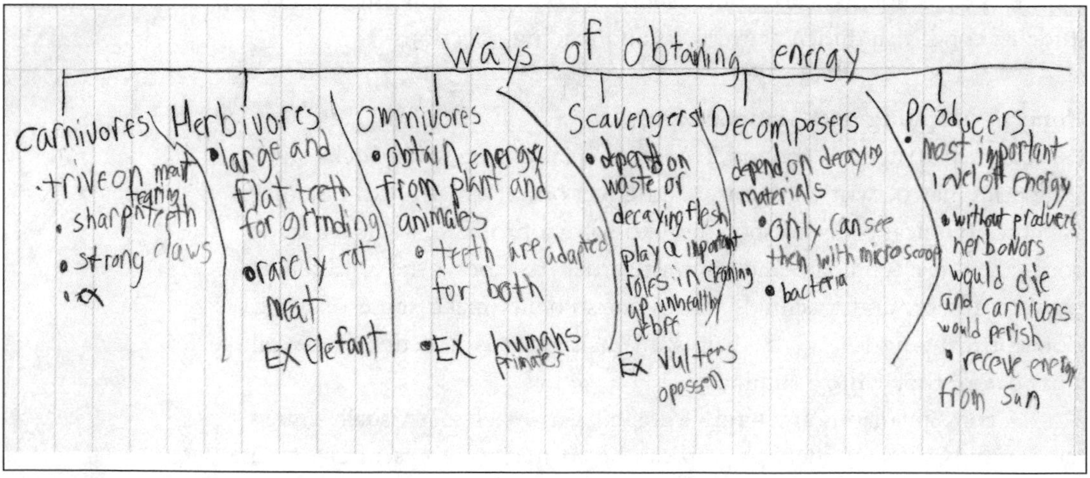

FIGURE 12–1. A tree map is a useful way to take notes on expository text.

Put a large box at the top of the page. We will write the topic in this box. Does anyone have an idea of the topic of the text? Brooke? Yes, *invasive species*. I wonder what that could mean. Then, we will make some smaller boxes to show the subtopics or supporting ideas. Can anyone use text features to find these supporting ideas?"... and so forth. After I have helped students to set up the tree map with the main ideas, they "partner read" the remainder of the text to fill in the details.

It would be fine to stop here. The concept map shows the main ideas and details, and students can use it for further discussion of the text. However, I have learned that it can be even more effective to go on and have students use the map to summarize the text. Analyzing the text to fill in the details on a concept map leaves students with a deconstructed version of the text. Ending with a written summary, on the other hand, requires students to reassemble the ideas into a whole. The summary can be written as a group, partner, or individual activity.

Concept mapping and summarizing can help students learn from content area texts. By drawing students' attention to the text structure and details of a text, concept maps lead students to a more developed understanding of the relationships between ideas.

Chapter Summary

- Summarizing, paraphrasing, and retelling can help students to cope with difficult content area readings.

- In order for students to remember what they learn, concepts must *make sense* and *have meaning*.

- Paraphrasing and retelling are forms of *elaborative rehearsal* that help learners to retain new information.

- Concept mapping and summarizing help students to see how ideas are related.

13 SUMMARIZING FOR ASSESSMENT

I hate grading. I put it off as long as possible. It seems that, no matter what marks I put at the top of the paper, students confuse my rating for the actual learning process. The task is no longer important; only my rating counts. When I put a B or a check or a seven out of ten on a student's paper, the grade is what they remember of the entire lesson or process. Even when I use a rubric, students scan over the criteria looking for points or an overall score.

I tried to avoid this outcome by only writing comments on student summaries. No grades, just statements of what students were doing well and what they needed to improve. Before I handed the summaries back to students, I explained what I had done and what I hoped they would learn. "And you will keep these summaries in your portfolios, so that next time you can look back at the comments to see what to improve."

About half an hour later, Chris came up to my desk. "Uh, Mrs. Kissner? You forgot to put a grade on this."

"I didn't give your summary a grade," I explained for what seemed the millionth time. "I only wrote down what you did well and what you need to change next time. For example, you did a nice job of recording main ideas, but you need to work on leaving out your own opinions."

"So it's a B?"

"It's not any grade," I said.

"A C, then?"

"It doesn't have a grade," I said slowly. "I just want to see you improve next time. Don't put in your own opinions, like you did here and here." I pointed to the lines in his summary.

"Oh," he said, and it seemed that comprehension dawned. But his next words showed otherwise. "So it's like a pretest, and you'll give me a grade next time."

Actually, this sounded like a pretty good idea. Students have trouble understanding what a letter grade or number represents. However, if I could come up with a concrete representation of progress, they might be able to understand their growth and learning.

I decided to use Chris' idea and assess two summaries: a baseline and a final. Both the students and I would be able to see improvement. Based on their strengths and weaknesses, I could also plan further instruction. Here are the steps I followed.

A Plan for Assessing Summarizing

Begin by carefully selecting the texts you plan to use. Be sure that both texts are similar in form, content, and style. Look for opportunities for students to collapse lists, find main ideas, delete trivia, and use key words. If you have students working in reading groups, you may decide to give students texts according to their reading levels. This can be an easy way to differentiate your instruction for students of differing abilities.

You may want to use the selections from earlier in this book, such as "Gardening with Native Plants" or "The American Chestnut." The article "Invasive Plants" would work when paired with these other texts (Figure 13–1), but texts from your regular curriculum are fine as well. If you are working with fiction, you can use chapters from a novel for the assessment process—a few chapters at the beginning of the novel and a few from the end.

After you have chosen your text, you can start the baseline assessment process. Simply hand out the text and ask students to write a summary. Use the checklist from earlier in the book to assess summaries and decide where to go with your instruction. When you feel that students are ready, use the paired text for the final assessment. To score the final summary, use the same checklist that you used before, but mark the scores with a different-colored pen. This provides an instant visual of whether students have improved.

The checklist becomes a helpful tool for sharing information with students and parents. Instead of simply a letter grade or number, students see that they have moved from "Beginning" to "Proficient." And if a student has not made progress, the checklist provides a good starting point for a discussion about what is not working in class.

Wanted: The Five Most Invasive Plants in the United States!

Warning: *These plants look pretty. They seem nice. But these nasty invaders are causing great harm to our native plants and animals. How do they do it? By taking over an area and choking out native plants, invasive plants upset the balance of an ecosystem.*

Invasive plants are plants that are not native to North America. They have arrived here in many ways. Some came with the first settlers, as seeds mixed in with the hay in their mattresses or stuck to the bottoms of their shoes. Some escaped from gardens or ponds where they were planted. No matter how they arrived, invasive plants spell big trouble for every ecosystem.

According to the Nature Conservancy, the plants below are the five worst offenders in North America.

Purple loosestrife

This pretty purple plant was once sold in nurseries and planted by gardeners. What's the problem? It can produce millions of seeds that spread by wind or water. Now it is found choking out wetlands all across the country. Stands of purple loosestrife can spread to be thousands of acres large. When it takes over a wetland area, this plant displaces native plants and disturbs animal habitats.

Kudzu

Kudzu is a climbing vine that can grow up to one foot each day. Once, kudzu was planted to control soil erosion. In the 1930s, young men working for the Civilian Conservation Corps planted acres of kudzu to try to conserve soil.

Unfortunately, kudzu quickly grew out of control. The thick vines and big leaves encircle native plants and smother them. Abandoned houses and vehicles have become covered by vines in the late summer.

Multiflora rose

When people think of roses, they often picture fragrant crimson blossoms flourishing in a pampered garden. Unfortunately, the multiflora rose is quite different from garden roses. Imported from Japan in 1886, this rose needs no

FIGURE 13–1.

gardener to help it spread quickly and form deep, thorny thickets. The multiflora rose thickets crowd out native species and compete with trees and other desirable plants for nutrients. Found on the edges of forests, roads, and fields, the shrub has clusters of white flowers that bloom in May and June. The fruits (called rose hips) are a favorite of birds, which then spread the seeds to allow more multiflora roses to grow.

Giant salvinia

Imagine a large, clear pond. One day two small green leaves appear on top. The next day, there are more green leaves. In a few weeks, the entire surface of the pond is covered with a green and brown mat of leaves. This is the work of the aquatic fern giant salvinia.

Brought from Brazil to be used in aquariums, the giant salvinia is not yet as widespread as the other invasive plants. Which is good news—for now. By covering the surfaces of streams, ponds, and lakes, the giant salvinia kills underwater plants, depletes the oxygen in the water, and wreaks havoc with the aquatic food chain. Scientists are working with local boaters and fishermen to identify outbreaks quickly and get rid of giant salvinia before it gets out of control.

Tree of heaven

The tree of heaven, or ailanthus, can grow in unfavorable locations with very little care. Introduced to the United States in 1784, this tree can produce up to 325,000 seeds in one year! It grows quickly, sometimes up to three feet per year. And because it will often "plant" itself in unlikely locations such as sidewalk cracks and flat-topped roofs, its roots can cause damage to sewers, building foundations, and other structures.

Besides causing damage, the tree of heaven also competes with native trees. It can produce toxins that are poisonous to other plant species. Once established, it will quickly overtake an area, crowding out the native species that other animals depend upon.

You can help native plants survive. If you notice any of the invasive plants growing in your yard, ask your parents for permission to remove them. When you choose plants for your garden, be sure to look for native plants. And never plant one of these invasive species around your house.

FIGURE 13–1. *Continued*

Peer Response

I can't give feedback about everything that a student writes. Luckily, I don't have to. Students can be effective critics of themselves and of one another. Peer response is yet another way to engage students in rich, detailed conversations about summarizing.

. . . or it can be a zoo. Peer response can be irritating, annoying, and bothersome, and that's just the part when the students choose partners. Intermediate students are not born critics. Without clear criteria and abundant modeling, kids often just sit back and say, "It was good."

How can we make peer response work? There are several roads to success. First of all, zoom in on one aspect of summarizing. Peer response is much more effective when students are focused on just one criterion. Giving students a specific action or task to complete as part of the peer response activity helps them to pay attention to the important elements. Next, pay attention to the processes. Students always beg to work with their friends, and often I allow it. Peer response is one time when it may be better to assign partners or groups. I learned that a careful structure is the secret to success.

It works fairly simply. Suppose students were coming to class with a completed summary. I plan the lesson by considering an aspect of summarizing that students need to work on. If I noticed that student summaries of fiction were lacking in character names and specific details, I choose to address this issue.

To keep myself from writing the same directions all the time, I made an overhead transparency entitled "Peer Response" to structure the lesson (Figure 13–2). I write my target criteria at the top of the page. When the students arrive, I teach a quick minilesson about the topic. Next, I walk around the room and collect the summaries from the students who are finished. Because I have yet to encounter a class in which every student completes every assignment, I isolate the students who did not finish the task by sending them elsewhere in the room. No fearful punishment awaits them; they just have to complete the summary! I redistribute the completed summaries to other students in the class. The entire process takes less time than assigning partners or allowing students to choose.

Every peer response session includes steps 1 and 2. I use Steps 3 and 4 to write the specific responses that students will make to the summary. If students are working with character names and specific text details, step 3 might read, "Circle the character names in the summary

Peer Response

Target Criteria:

Directions

1. Sign your name at the bottom of the summary you received.

2. Read the summary carefully. Write one positive comment about the summary.

3.

4.

5. Write one suggestion for the author.

6. Return the summary to its author.

7. Read the comments on your summary and make revisions.

FIGURE 13–2.

you are reading," and step 4 could be, "Put a star in a location that you think needs a character name." In step 5, students write a suggestion for the author, and in step 6, they return the summaries to their owners. At the end of the process, students use the advice from their peers to revise their summaries. I talk students through the revisions. "If you do not have any character names circled, what does that tell you about your summary? Where can you make some changes?"

Students enjoy seeing the comments of their peers, and the specific responses help them to see how to improve their work. I alter the specific response strategies as needed for different classes. (Some groups love to use those highlighters!) See the specific suggestions (Figure 13–3) for student problems for more ideas about peer response.

Problem in Student Summary	*Actions for Peer Response*
Too many words	Circle at least 10 words that can be eliminated
Copying directly from the text	Highlight phrases that come from the text
Irrelevant details	Highlight details that do not contribute to the main idea
Repeated ideas	Circle repeated words or phrases
Not including important ideas	Put a star above every main idea from the text
Ideas not connected	Circle connection words in the summary
Key words not included	Make a list of key words from the text; highlight the words that appear in the summary

FIGURE 13–3. Ideas for Specific Peer Response

Always Allow Access to the Text

When you assess student summaries, there are some important factors to keep in mind. Be sure that students have access to the original text when they summarize. If the text is removed, the assessment is more of the student's memory than of summarizing skill.

It's good practice for students to have frequent experience in looking back to the text. Because no one recalls 100 percent of what they read, the brain fills in the gaps through a process called *confabulation*. It is an unconscious process, and the reader does not know which details are accurate and which are fabricated. Therefore, allowing students to go back to the text lets them check on details to be sure they are accurate. (Sousa 2001).

Chapter Summary

- Plan to assess summarizing by choosing two similar texts. Each text should have opportunities for students to collapse lists, find main ideas, delete trivia, and use key words.

- Use different colored pens to mark students' proficiency with the baseline and final assessment. This way, students can see if they have improved.

- To make peer response successful, choose specific criteria for response. Be sure to communicate clear guidelines for the response process.

- Always allow students to use the text during the summarizing process.

Assessing summaries can be a difficult task. Looking at progress over time and giving opportunities for peer response helps the classroom teacher to make the best assessments of student growth.

Conclusion

The more I learned about summarizing, paraphrasing, and retelling, the more I became committed to using these processes to help my students make meaning of what they read. In middle school and elementary school, in reading classes or content area classes, these skills are valuable for students of all reading levels and all abilities.

I started out looking for some quick activities to add to my daily instruction, some new information to add to conversations with other teachers. I found much more. If students are to become competent, responsible learners, able to digest and synthesize all the information that comes their way, they must know how to put ideas into their own words. They must be able to tell someone else what they have read, summarize details from a variety of sources, find what is important in a text, and communicate that idea to someone else.

What do these processes look like in the classroom? I see glimpses of summarizing, paraphrasing, and retelling each day. Jacob writes notes to himself about how to use the distributive property in math class. Melissa and Jamie struggle with how to condense four weeks of research with acids and bases into one paragraph. Thomas tells Corey what he missed during yesterday's read-aloud. And sometimes, students turned the tables and challenged me to summarize.

"Why do you want this piece of writing, Mrs. Kissner?" Brooke asked, and I told her offhandedly that I was writing a book about summarizing.

Instantly all of the students around us were intrigued. "What? Tell us about it."

"Am I in it?" Scott demanded. "Am I?" asked Sean. "What's it about?" questioned Julie. "Wait a second." Brian held up his hand and the rest of the students were quiet. A mischievous smile spread on his face. "Why don't you summarize it for us, Mrs. Kissner?"

References

Anderson, V., and S. Hidi. 1989. "Teaching Students to Summarize." *Educational Leadership* 46: 26–28.

Aulls, M. W. 1975. "Expository Paragraph Properties that Influence Literal Recall." *Journal of Reading Behavior* 7: 391–400.

Benson, V., and C. Cummins. 2000. *The Power of Retelling: Developmental Steps for Building Comprehension.* Bothell, WA: Wright Group McGraw-Hill.

Brown, A., and J. Day. 1983. "Macrorules for Summarizing Texts: The Development of Expertise." *Journal of Verbal Learning and Verbal Behavior* 22: 1–14.

Burns, P., B. Roe, and E. Ross. 1996. *Teaching Reading in Today's Elementary Schools.* Boston: Houghton Mifflin.

Carnine, L., and D. Carnine. 2004. "The Interaction of Reading Skills and Science Content Knowledge When Teaching Struggling Secondary Students." *Reading and Writing Quarterly* 20: 203–18.

Clark, K., and M. Graves. 2005. "Scaffolding Students' Comprehension of Text." *The Reading Teacher* 58 (6): 570–80.

Coleman, E., A. Brown, and I. Rivkin. 1997. "The Effect of Instructional Explanations on Learning from Scientific Texts." *Journal of the Learning Sciences* 6: 347–62.

Davey, B., and D. Miller. 1990. "Topicalization and the Processing of Expository Prose by Children: Mediating Effects of Cognitive Styles and Content Familiarity." *Educational Psychology* 10: 23–38.

Davis, M., and R. Hult. 1997. "Effects of Writing Summaries as a Generative Learning Activity During Note Taking." *Teaching of Psychology* 24: 47–49.

Davis, Z. 1994. "Effects of Prereading Story Mapping on Elementary Readers' Comprehension." *Journal of Educational Research* 87: 6.

Fazio, B. B., R. C. Naremore, and P. J. Connell. 1996. "Tracking Children from Poverty at Risk for Specific Language Impairment: A Three-Year Longitudinal Study." *Journal of Speech and Hearing Research* 39: 611–24.

Feldt, R. C., R. A. Feldt, and K. Kilburg. 2002. "Acquisition, Maintenance, and Transfer of a Questioning Strategy in Second and Third Grade Students to Learn from Science Textbooks." *Reading Psychology* 23: 181–98.

Fisk, C., and B. Hurst. 2003. "Paraphrasing for Comprehension." *The Reading Teacher* 57: 182–95.

Fitzgerald, J., D. L. Spiegel, and T. B. Webb. 1985. "Development of Children's Knowledge of Story Structure and Content." *Journal of Educational Research* 79: 101–08.

Friend, R. 2000. "Teaching Summarization as a Content Area Reading Strategy." *Journal of Adolescent and Adult Literacy* 4: 320–29.

Gambrell, L., P. Koskinen, and B. Kapinus. 1991. "Retelling and the Reading Comprehension of Proficient and Less-Proficient Readers." *Journal of Educational Research* 84: 356–62.

Gambrell, L., W. Pfeiffer, and R. Wilson. 1985. "The Effects of Retelling Upon Reading Comprehension and Recall of Text Information." *Journal of Educational Research* 78: 216–20.

Garner, R., M. Gillingham, and S. White. 1989. "Effects of 'Seductive Details' on Macroprocessing and Microprocessing of Adults and Children." *Cognition and Instruction* 6: 41–57.

Hahn, A., and R. Garner. 1985. "Synthesis of Research on Students' Ability to Summarize Text." *Educational Leadership* 42: 52–55.

Hidi, S., and V. Anderson. 1986. "Producing Written Summaries: Task Demands, Cognitive Operations, and Implications for Instruction." *Review of Educational Research* 56: 473–93.

Hidi, S., W. Baird, and A. Hildyard. 1982. "That's Important But Is It Interesting? Two Factors in Text Processing." In *Discourse Processing*, edited by A. Flammer and W. Kintsch, 63–75. Amsterdam, Netherlands: North-Holland.

Kintsch, E. 1990. "Macroprocesses and Microprocesses in the Development of Summarization Skill." *Cognition and Instruction* 7: 161–95.

Maas, D. 2002. "Make Your Paraphrasing Plagiarism-Proof with a Coat of E-Prime." *Education* 59: 196–205.

Meyer, B. J. F. 1985. "Prose Analysis: Purpose, Procedures, and Problems." In *Understanding Expository Text*, edited by B. K. Britton, and J. B. Black. Hillsdale, NJ: Lawrence Erlbaum Associates. 11–64, 269–97.

Meyer, B. J. F., D. M. Brandt, and G. J. Bluth. 1980. "Use of the Top-Level Structure in Text: Key for Reading Comprehension of Ninth Grade Students." *Reading Research Quarterly* 1: 72–103.

Pearce, C. 1999. *Nurturing Inquiry*. Portsmouth, NH: Heinemann.

Rhoder, Carol. 2002. "Mindful Reading: Strategy Instruction That Facilitates Transfer." *Journal of Adolescent & Adult Literacy* 45: 198–213.

Ruddell, R., and O. Boyle. 1989. "A Study of Cognitive Mapping as a Means to Improve Summarization and Comprehension of Expository Text." *Reading Research and Instruction* 29: 12–22.

Sjostrom, C. L., and V. C. Hare. 1984. "Teaching High School Students to Identify Main Ideas in Expository Text." *Journal of Educational Research* 78: 114–18.

Sousa, D. A. 2001. *How the Brain Learns: A Classroom Teacher's Guide*. Thousand Oaks, CA: Corwin Press.

Taylor, K. K. 1986. "Summary Writing by Young Children." *Reading Research Quarterly* 21: 193–207.

Uemlianan, I. 2000. "Engaging Text: Assessing Paraphrase and Understanding." *Studies in Higher Education* 25: 347.

USFWS. *The Karner Blue Butterfly*. Available at http:northeast.fws.gov/factshee.html. Accessed April 13, 2005.

Vacca, R., and J. A. Vacca. 2002. *Content Area Reading: Literacy and Learning Across the Curriculum*. Boston: Allyn & Bacon.

van Dijk, T. A, and W. Kintsch. 1978. "Toward a Model of Text Comprehension and Production." *Psychological Review* 85: 363–94.

Wagner, C. R., B. Sahlen, and U. Nettelblat. 1999. "What's the Story? Narration and Comprehension in Swedish Children with Language Impairment." *Child Language Teaching and Therapy* 15: 113–38.

Winograd, P. 1984. "Strategic Differences in Summarizing Texts." *Reading Research Quarterly* 19: 404–25.

Picture Books

Bliss, C. D. 1992. *Matthew's Meadow.* New York: Harcourt.

Cherry, L. 1992. *A River Ran Wild.* San Diego: Gulliver Green Book.

Creech, S. 1994. *Walk Two Moons.* New York: HarperCollins.

George, J. C. 1997. *Everglades.* New York: HarperCollins.

Hayes, J. 1993. *Soft Child: How Rattlesnake Got Its Fangs.* Tucson: Harbinger.

Hermes, P. 2001. *Westward to Home: Joshua's Diary, The Oregon Trail, 1948 (My America).* New York: Scholastic.

Hollenbeck, K. 1999. *Dancing on the Sand: A Story of an Atlantic Blue Crab.* Norwalk, CT: Soundprints.

Jimenez, F. 1997. *The Circuit: Stories from the Life of a Migrant Child.* Albuquerque: University of New Mexico Press.

O'Brien, R. C. 1995. *The Secret of Nimh.* New York: Scholastic.

Paulsen, G. 1990. *Woodsong.* New York: Bradbury Press.

Sachar, L. 1998. *Holes.* New York: Farrar, Straus and Giroux.

Schuett, S. 1997. *Somewhere in the World Right Now.* New York: Knopf.

Siebert, D. 1996. *Sierra.* New York: HarperTrophy.

Sturges, P. 1998. *Bridges Are to Cross.* New York: Putnam.

Yolen, J. 1995. *Letting Swift River Go.* Boston: Little Brown.